The Cash Family
Scrapbook

The Cash Family Scrapbook

Cindy Cash

INTRODUCTION BY JOHNNY CASH

Crown Trade Paperbacks
New York

Published by Crown Trade Paperbacks, Inc., 201 East 50th Street, New York, New York 10022. Member of the Crown Publishing Group.

Random House, Inc. New York, Toronto, London, Sydney, Auckland
http://www.randomhouse.com/

CROWN TRADE PAPERBACKS and colophon are trademarks of Crown Publishers, Inc.

Printed in the United States of America

Design by Blonde *on* Pond

Library of Congress Cataloging-in-Publication Data

Cash, Cindy
The Cash family scrapbook/ by Cindy Cash; introduction by Johnny Cash.
1. Cash, Johnny. 2. Country musicians—United States—Biography.
I. Cash, Johnny. II. Title.
ML420.C265C37   1997
782.42'1642'092—dc20
              [B]   96-24495
                    MN

ISBN 0-517-88723-1

10 9 8 7 6 5 4 3 2 1

First Edition

This book is dedicated to my mother, Vivian.
She has been the constant, daily stability throughout my life.
I believe my mother has earned this dedication.
I love you, Mom.

Acknowledgments

SPECIAL THANKS: To my dad, thank you for your friendship, your wisdom, your wit, your music, your love, and for letting me catch more fish than you . . . I love you, too. To my sisters, Rosanne, Kathy, and Tara, who are three of my best girlfriends. I'm grateful I had three extra hands to hold. To my daughter, Jessica. You are the one true love of my life. To my brother, John Carter. As children we lived in two different worlds, but sharing a father brought us together in one. I'm glad you're my brother. To my grandmothers, Irene Liberto and Carrie Cloveree Cash, for your strength of womanhood. To my grandfathers, Tom Liberto and Ray Cash, for the stories you left to be told.

Additional thanks to: Karen Adams (a special thanks for your friendship and your time and input, which added to this book); Lisa Trice; Kelly Hancock; Bill Miller; Bob Sullivan and Rene Swope; Ana Maria Alessa; Lou Robin; Hugh Waddell; Lee Bookman and Kate Dominus at the Agency for the Performing Arts; Ron Keith, Arleen Johnston, Linda Mason, and Arlene Chadwick (for listening); Ricardo Fields and Alicia Armstrong for your support; Jerry Sharp for your sweet love; and to my entire family—past, present, and future.

Introduction

By Johnny Cash

FROM THE TIME Cindy was a baby, she and I have been very close. There's been a bond that's sweet and rare. She was always the first person I'd hear from when coming home from a tour, and usually I'd get messages at hotels where I stayed to "call Cindy at home."

One day when she was no more than four years old and we were living in Casitas Springs, California, on the side of a mountain, I decided to go for a climb. I loved to climb that mountain. I was three or four hundred yards up the side of the mountain above the house with my ropes and tools when I heard Cindy crying. I looked down and there she was, halfway to me, and holding on with all her might. I descended and took her in my arms and carried her back down. When I asked her why she had followed me, she said simply that she wanted to go with me.

I was gone most of the time during her childhood years and when she was nine, her mother and I were divorced, and to Cindy and me both, it was a terrible truth: "Daddy stopped coming home."

I visited as often as possible and we spent some wonderful summers together, she and her three sisters, in Tennessee, water-skiing, fishing, and camping.

It was when she became a teenager that I realized that of all the girls, Cindy was most like me. She loved the out-of-doors, and I taught her to shoot, just for fun, at targets. I taught her to fish using a spinning reel, and this she mastered. From the time I taught her she always caught more fish than I did.

I taught her a couple of chords on the guitar and she started writing songs. She took some of her beautiful poems as well, and sang them.

Her mind opened up like a flower as she became a young woman. Her spiritual world awoke and she had a really spiritual experience and made a strong commitment to God.

Though she became worldwise as well as streetwise, she holds to many traditional and fundamental values when it comes to family, relationships, and God.

Her heart and soul are always bared in her poetry. She'll often call me up and say, "Dad, listen to this," and I'm always amazed at her intellectual, spiritual, and emotional depth. Through her poems is revealed the beauty of her soul. These pieces of her writing alone make this book worthwhile.

She must have kept every picture she has ever had of everyone in our enormous family, including these pictures of me, published here for the first time. Some of the pictures, going back three or four generations, were supplied by other family members, such as myself, but most of them are Cindy's.

From the Cash side, I would like to include a little history as well as a possible vignette or two from earlier generations.

Cindy's great-grandfather, William Henry Cash, left Elbert County, Georgia, in a mule-drawn wagon following the loss of the family home and property, which came about as the result of Union General William T. Sherman's fiery march through Georgia.

Six-year-old William Henry rode the wagon with his family to the rich farmland of Cleveland County, Arkansas, where the family homesteaded. He was one of twelve children, and would eventually come to marry and father twelve children himself, of which Cindy's grandfather (my father), Ray Cash, would be the baby.

Dad.

William Henry went into the Gospel Ministry at an early age, and after being ordained a Baptist minister, rode a horse and carried a Bible and gun as a circuit-riding preacher, holding services at several churches every week, scattered out in the rural areas of Cleveland County. He was truly dedicated, for in all his many years in the ministry, he never took money. He did, however, receive lots of love offerings, such as meat, eggs, chickens, vegetables, and various foods he used to feed his large family.

Cindy's grandfather, my father, was born in 1897. When William Henry Cash died at an early age in 1912 of Parkinson's disease—or Bell's palsy, as it was called then—my father supported his mother by farming cotton until she died in 1916. Then he joined the army.

Stationed out of Deming, New Mexico, he served with General John J. Pershing's forces and was part of the troop sent to try to capture the Mexican guerrilla leader Pancho Villa after he burned Columbus, New Mexico.

Later, Ray Cash was sent to France but, thankfully, the Armistice was signed before he saw any action.

He returned home and married Carrie Rivers on August 18, 1920. In courting my mother, he rode a horse every

Sunday from Rison Community, where he lived, to her home in Crossroads Community, not far from Kingsland, Arkansas.

My father often told the story of his courtship. It seems that the boys around Crossroads had decided that this stranger was not going to court Carrie Rivers anymore. Crossroads was about four miles down a gravel road from Kingsland in heavily wooded country. One Sunday afternoon, four young men stepped out of the woods and stopped my father. One of them took hold of the horse's bridle and said, "You are not going to see Carrie Rivers anymore. Turn around and go back and stay out of this country or we're going to kill you."

My father took a pistol out from under his coat and said, "I've got six bullets in this gun. That's more than enough to get all of you. Now back up and don't ever bother me anymore." The boys did as he said and he went on his way.

After he married my mother, my father farmed on Grandpa Rivers's place for years. I was born there in an old house on his property on February 26, 1932. The house sat just off the gravel road, surrounded by tall pine trees.

I was born midmorning as my father planted potatoes in the field behind the house, and according to my dad, there was a heavy snow which covered the field as he planted.

There was no doctor attending my delivery. I was the fourth child and no doctor was sent for. A midwife came by, a lady named Easterling; and a distant cousin, knowing that my mother's time was at hand, helped with my delivery.

My father came in from the field when Mrs. Easterling called out to him, "You have a son." My father looked at me, made some offhand comment about me not being too pretty, and seeing that my mother was in pain went looking for the doctor.

He found him down on the river fishing, and as my father tells it, old Doctor Johnson came in the house, looked at my mother, and said, "I'll give you something for pain." He had his fishing worms in the same pocket in which he carried the aspirin. So he picked two aspirins out of the handful of worms and handed them to Mrs. Easterling to give to my mother, which she did not do.

My father returned to the field, and before sundown my mother was back on her feet cooking supper for my father and my siblings.

Cindy comes from strong pioneer stock. In her poems and songs she exposes the pain and suffering as well as the joy and celebration of life. She has known hard times of a different nature from those of her ancestors, but she shows that trouble and strife come to us all; whether it's the disappointment of a failed crop because of a flood or a failed love affair, she tells a human story with her writings and her pictures, a story of love that has brought her through her hard times. As this scrapbook of vignettes of her life makes clear, the love and companionship of her family, grounded in great faith in God, makes her feel that eventually everybody, including Daddy, is coming home.

Preface

JOHNNY CASH WAS born on February 26, 1932. He was the fourth of seven children born to Ray and Carrie Cash in Dyess, Arkansas. His life is documented in his own words in his autobiography, *Man in Black*.

In *The Cash Family Scrapbook* you will find out about the parts of his life I am most familiar with as his daughter. This includes his personal and professional life as a father, husband, grandfather, friend, singer, songwriter, musician, author, journalist, photographer, patriarch, ordained minister, Christian, and humanitarian.

I will share with you photographs that have never been seen before outside my family, short stories on important moments or incidents, letters written while on the road, poetry I've written over the years for my family, lists of accomplishments, and a personal look at the "family man" provided by those who know him best.

I would now like to introduce you to a new side of Johnny Cash and his family. His given name is J. R.

Me.

Cash. When he joined the air force, they required a first name, and he chose John. It then became John R. Cash. My mom called him Johnny and it was used as his professional name. In these pages you will meet not only J. R. Cash, but also John Cash, aka Grandpa, aka Dad.

The Cash Family Scrapbook

ℳom and Dad Meet

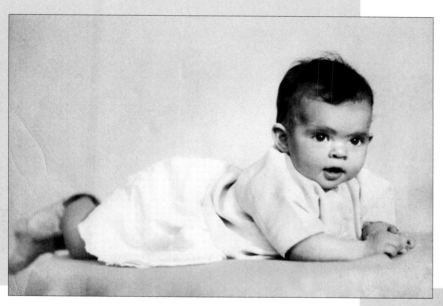

Mom's baby photo.

Mom's senior class photo.

My mother was born Vivian Dorraine Liberto. She was the middle child—after her brother, Ray, and before her sister, Sylvia—born to Irene and Tom Liberto of San Antonio.

She was reared in a strict Catholic environment and was a straight-A student all through school. From what I know about her childhood, her father, who owned an insurance company, was the predominant parent while she was growing up. He was a good man. I was ten years old when he died and have only fond memories of him. He was very dedicated to his family. He died in 1969.

My grandmother was the quiet and gentle type. After Grandpa died, she moved to California, where she lived with us until her death in 1978.

I have fond memories of her as well. My mother was very devoted to both of them—as she is to my sisters and me and all our children.

My dad was stationed at Brooks Air Force Base in San Antonio when he met my mother in 1951. They met at a roller-skating rink. Mom was skating and Dad accidentally knocked her down. It was love at first sight. Literally.

Dad asked her if he could see her home on the bus. She was spending the night with a girlfriend. While they were on the bus, he tried to kiss her, but she wouldn't let him. However, she did give him her phone number and they dated for the next thirty days, until Dad was sent to Landsberg, Germany, where he was to be stationed for the next three years.

They corresponded through the mail regularly, and after about a year and a half, he proposed. She accepted and he sent her an engagement ring in the mail. They were married immediately upon his return at St. Ann's Catholic Church in San Antonio, on August 7, 1954.

Their wedding night was spent somewhere between Texas and Memphis. They settled in an apartment in Memphis while Dad sold appliances door-to-door trying to provide for his new wife. He despised his job. He knew it was probably time to work harder on his music career when he rang the last doorbell of a long, unsuccessful day and greeted the housewife with, "You don't want to buy a vacuum cleaner, do you?"

Mom became pregnant one month after they were married, having spent the first month of her marriage crying because she wanted to become pregnant immediately. She wanted children desperately. Shortly after the news of her pregnancy, Dad was signed to Sun Records and had his first single released.

Rosanne was born May 24, 1955. When she was one month old, Dad was booked on his first out-of-state tour, to Texas. Mom said that she cried every night the whole week he was gone. They had never been separated since their wedding night and she had no phone and no car. She felt so alone.

This was to be the beginning of a lifetime of touring for Dad and many more nights alone for Mom.

Mom and Dad.

Mom.

Mom and Dad with Mom's uncle, Father Vincent
Liberto, who performed the wedding ceremony.

A New Bride and a New Career

Front of fan club membership card.

Membership in National

JOHNNY CASH
FAN CLUB
This card entitles the bearer

to all membership privileges of the Fan Club
from 1961 to 1962.

Annual membership, $1.25

President
Honorary Pres.
Address: P. O. Box 5056   Memphis, Tenn.

Back of fan club membership card.

Early publicity—Dad.

Early publicity—Dad.

Mom and Dad with our parrot, Jethro.
He could say "Mama" just like us girls. He could
laugh, cry, call our names, and was a part of the
family for many years.

Mom and Dad as
newlyweds at home
in Memphis.

In this photo Mom looked so much like Rosanne does today to me. February 21, 1957, Las Vegas, Nevada.

Backstage somewhere. Mom and Dad.

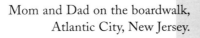

Mom and Dad on the boardwalk, Atlantic City, New Jersey.

Dad, Mom, Rosanne, and Kathy.

Dad soaking
up the sun.

Mom and Dad
while living on
Havenhurst in
Encino, California.

Dad and Elvis. They always had a good time together.

Dad and Elvis, December 22, 1957.

24

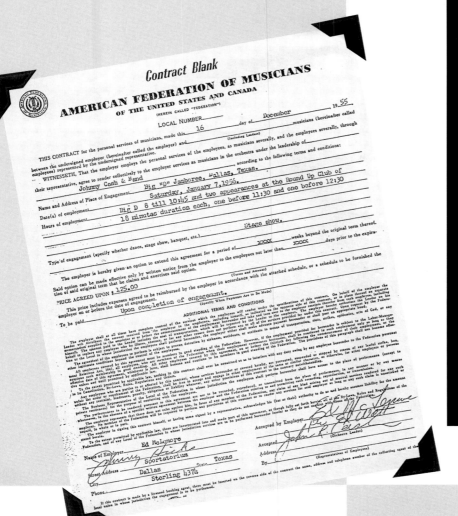

It was Memphis 1955 on Union Avenue." At least that's what he said in the song "I Will Rock and Roll with You."

Union Avenue was a frequently traveled road in 1955. It was the street Sun Records sat on, and many young men knocked on the company's door to sell their songs. Elvis Presley, Jerry Lee Lewis, Carl Perkins, and Johnny Cash walked through that door and walked back out, soon to be called the Million-Dollar Quartet.

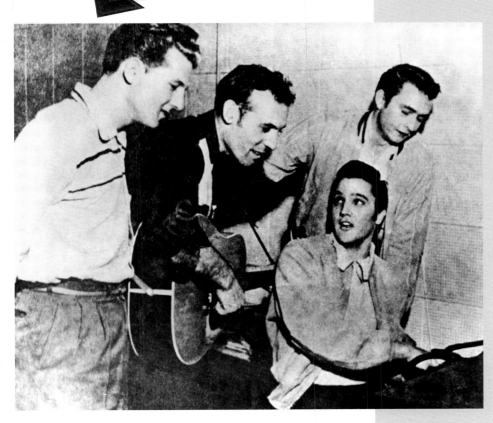

The Million-Dollar Quartet: Jerry Lee Lewis, Carl Perkins, Dad, and Elvis Presley (at the piano). This was taken during a recording session of Carl's. The other three just happened by.

I Walk the Line

I keep a close watch on this heart of mine

I keep my eyes wide open all the time

I keep the ends out for the tie that binds

Because you're mine, I walk the line

I find it very, very easy to be true

I find myself alone when each day is through

Yes, I'll admit that I'm a fool for you

Because you're mine, I walk the line

As sure as night is dark and day is light

I keep you on my mind both day and night

And happiness I've known proves that it's right

Because you're mine, I walk the line

You've got a way to keep me on your side

You give me cause for love that I can't hide

For you I know I'd even try to turn the tide

Because you're mine, I walk the line

I keep a close watch on this heart of mine

I keep my eyes wide open all the time

I keep the ends out for the tie that binds

Because you're mine, I walk the line

$\mathcal{M}$y Oldest Sister, Rosanne, Arrives May 24, 1955

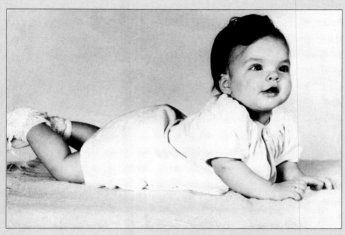

Rosanne Cash.

Rosanne.

Dad and Rosanne.

When Rosanne was only six weeks old, Mom became pregnant with Kathy. During this time, she and Dad bought their first house, on Tutwiler Avenue in Memphis. Dad was well into his singing career and was on the road a lot now. He was opening "The Elvis Presley Show" and was a well-known "rockabilly."

Dad and Rosanne at the Memphis Zoo in 1956.

Rosanne.

Mom and Rosanne.

Rosanne.

Kathy Arrives

Kathy was born April 16, 1956, in Memphis. Rosanne was only ten and a half months old when Kathy was born. Mom had her hands full.

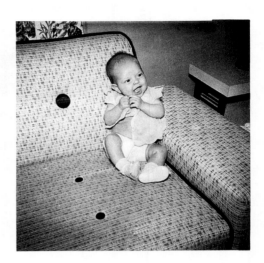

Kathy.

Kathy Cash.

Kathy.

Rosanne feeding Kathy her bottle.

Rosanne and Kathy, Easter 1958.

Mom holding Rosanne
and Kathy, Easter.

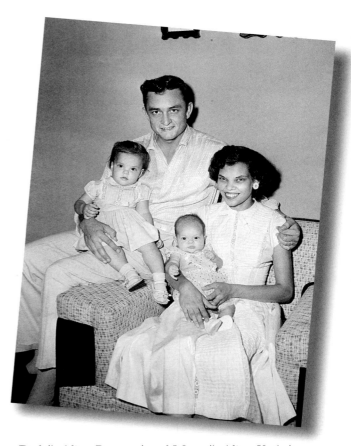

Dad (holding Rosanne) and Mom (holding Kathy).

This is my favorite photo of my parents. Dad leaves again, but this time, Mom doesn't have to stay home. The trip was a dream come true for them both: a few days in Ireland.

Mom and Dad at home.

I always thought Dad made a handsome cowboy.

Kathy in high chair; Rosanne is watching out for her (she was always the little mother to us all).

Dad in costume for some of his early acting. This one was for "The Rebel."

Mom and Dad at home in Encino, California.

Cindy Arrives July 29, 1958

I was born in Memphis on July 29, 1958. Dad and Mom called me a "rockabilly baby" because I slept in a dresser drawer until I was six weeks old. We were moving out of Memphis.

Dad was to become involved in an acting career, so we packed up and moved to Hollywood. We bought Johnny Carson's house on Coldwater Canyon. I was then moved from a drawer to a crib.

MAY 59

Me.

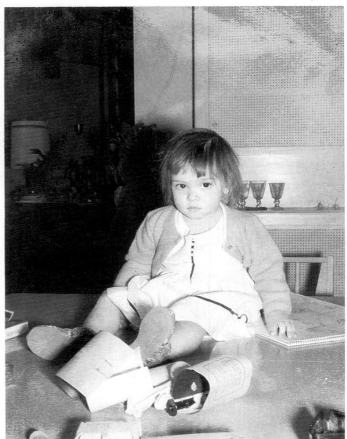

Me.

MAY • 59

MAY • 59

Kathy, me, and Rosanne.

Kathy, Rosanne, and me
(trying to get away).

L to R: Rosanne, Dad, Kathy,
and Mom (holding me).

After living in Hollywood for three years, Mom and Dad decided they wanted out of the city. We had some friends, Carol and Curly Lewis, who lived in Oak View, California (about sixty-five miles north of Los Angeles).

Curly was a contractor. He had located a mountainside in Casitas Springs, a tiny town eleven miles east of Ventura, California, next to Oak View. This mountainside was chosen because no other houses could ever be built on it, except ours, because of the lay of the land.

Our house was a large, one-level, ranch-style home with four bedrooms and a maid's quarters off to the side.

We always had a live-in maid. Looking back, I think it was because Mom would get a little lonely and a bit uneasy on that mountain with Dad always on the road, and she enjoyed the company of another adult.

I remember Mom constantly cleaning and cooking, even though she had a housekeeper. I never saw her in front of the television set or just lying around. She was always doing something, and my sisters and I also had several daily chores.

Our house was secluded, with no close neighbors; luckily, it was equipped with a huge playhouse out back, several pets, a barbecue pit, and a large pasture with a barn and three horses.

My first real memory is standing by my mom watching the construction of this home take place. I was three years old and Mom stood pregnant with Tara, my youngest sister.

Tara was born in Encino on August 24, 1961, and we moved into the house in Casitas Springs shortly thereafter. This is where we lived until 1968.

Me, Kathy, and Rosanne.

Living on Havenhurst Boulevard in Encino, California, in 1958. Rosanne is in front, Dad is holding me, Mom is holding Kathy and our pet spider monkey, Homer.

Home

There's a place in my heart

That I still call my own

Although out of my grasp

It will always be home

It sits high on a hill

Far away from the world

Where I was at peace

When I was a girl

When Santa was real

And Daddy was home

When Mama would smile

And a room of my own

When hearts were full

And love was free

And children were all

We would ever be

CINDY CASH—AGE 20

Tara Arrives
August 24, 1961

Once Tara was born we didn't experience the thrill of taking and watching home movies so frequently, so I thought it only fair to include a few extra baby photos of her. She was so cute.

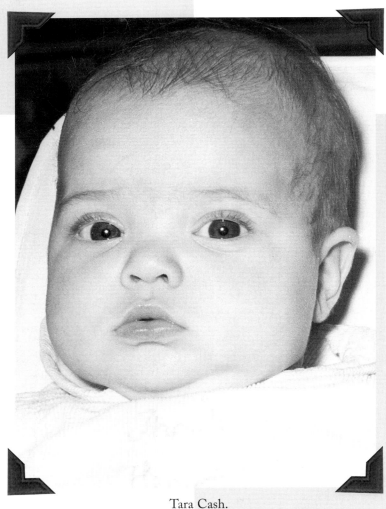

Tara Cash.

Rosanne holding Tara.

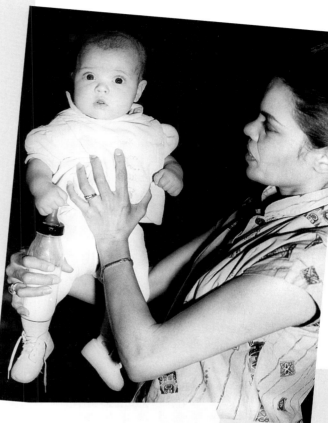

Mom
holding
Tara.

Tara at Easter.

Kathy, Rosanne, and Tara (in background).

Kathy holding Tara.

Dad and W. S. "Fluke" Holland.

Miss Tara

Dad wrote this song for Tara when she was twelve.

Where are you going, Miss Tara, Miss Tara

Where are you going, Miss Tara Joan

Yesterday when you played on the swing and the trampoline

You were already thinking of a life of your own

And I turn around twice and you're already gone

Who will you marry, Miss Tara, Miss Tara

Who will you marry, Miss Tara Joan

Will he have wealth and will he have fame

I'm sure, too, you're wondering just who he will be

Well, that's your decision, it's not up to me

I hope you'll be happy, Miss Tara, Miss Tara

I hope you'll be happy, Miss Tara Joan

And that you will stay with me till you're a woman

And wise to the world before you're off on your own

You're my last baby girl and I'll be so alone

Me, Rosanne, Mom (holding Tara), and Kathy.
An obvious publicity shot.

Tara, Rosanne, me, and Kathy.

Me, Kathy, and Rosanne. All of us had very
straight hair except Tara. Mom would roll our
hair every night in those pink sponge rollers
until we were in fifth or sixth grade and we
were old enough to rebel.

Rosanne, Kathy, Mom (holding Tara), and me.

Me at Easter.

Here I am again.

Me, Kathy and Tara in wagon, and Rosanne, in charge, at our house in Casitas Springs.

Please Come Home

I couldn't wait to learn how to read and write when I entered the first grade. I remember how badly I wanted to write letters to Dad whenever he left home to go on the road. I would feel like he'd forget about me if I didn't send him letters to remind him that I was waiting for him at home.

When I reached my midtwenties, Mom started giving my sisters and me memorabilia she had saved from our childhoods, some of these being the letters I had written to Dad. I don't believe they were ever mailed to him because of his constant traveling. He was usually in a different city every day, which obviously made it difficult for Mom to mail the letters while trying to calculate their arrivals to coincide with his arrivals.

However, I wrote him as often as I could. I was asking him to please come home.

One my mom saved I wrote when I was six.

1964

Dear Daddy,
is it cold or hot
there? I Love you
and I want you to
come home. Will you
be home for Hall-
oween I hope so.
LOVE Cindy

The Red Wagon. Me and Tara (me in wagon).

I pulled her everywhere that wagon would take us.

She tried pulling me.

It didn't work.

Me and Tara.

The four of us girls were all named by Dad. He chose not to give any of us a middle name. He figured if we didn't have one, nobody could call us by anything other than our given names.

We were all baptized in the Catholic Church, and during Tara's baptism, the priest informed Mom and Dad that Tara was not a saint's name and that she must be given a middle name on her baptism certificate in order for him to continue.

Dad said the only saint's name he could think of, at the time, was Joan of Arc. To this day Tara is Tara Joan Cash, but only on her baptism certificate.

Dad—Columbia Records, 1962.

Mom's Poetry

I'm not bad to look at

I've been a loving wife

Have done all I know to do

And for You, I'd give my life.

I've had four children for him

All which are beauties and smart

If only his love was for them

The five of us would not have

a broken heart.

He is blessed with goodness and talent

For some reason God let him stray

It's hard to

The hours I've spent

waiting for you

Would total a lifetime of a child.

The miles I've walked

The clocks I've watched

You'd never believe to be true.

The prayers I've said would

Reach from Earth to the sky.

VIVIAN CASH—1962

Mom has never been a singer or performer of any kind. As far as I know, she has never written any songs or poetry as a rule. However, when a person is in a lot of emotional pain and they are left to deal with it, sometimes writing it down helps them to accept it and maybe understand it just a little better. I'm an example.

In talking with my mom about this family album, she revealed to me that when I was a baby, she wrote a song about my dad and their life together at the time. She never put music to it or even completed it, but I felt that it was so important to let me include it that she agreed to let me print it.

The song clearly interprets the pain and frustration she endured while trying to raise small children alone and deal with her husband's career and the lifestyle that went along with it.

I thank her for allowing me to share this writing with the public. It appears here exactly as it was written, unfinished and heartfelt.

Dear God, hear my plea

And answer me.

It's not the life he wants to lead.

Deep inside he's good as gold

Lead him down the right road.

He's had it hard most of his life

And now he can't take it in his stride.

A lot has happened to change his thinking

Give him strength and promote his ranking.

He's got so much to live for

All that You have given him.

Don't let him down, Lord

He needs You and also them.

It would be easier for You to take his life

And let the kids proudly carry his name

Than to lose him to another wife

And all to have to live in shame.

Dear God, hear my plea

And answer me.

It's not the life he wants to lead.

He always tries to do what's right

And has the best intentions

But always old man Satan

Steps in to play his part.

I ask You please in the Lord's name

Come to our rescue

I know You won't let him live in shame

I'm on my knees to beg you.

VIVIAN CASH—1960

Carl Perkins and Dad on the road.

Early publicity—
Dad.

Early career photo of Dad.

Early publicity
shot of Dad.

The Birthday Dream

Close your eyes and dream with me

Of years gone by that made us be

Of years that turned our lives around

And gave us time to stand our ground

Close your eyes and dream of home

The safest place you've ever known

Close your eyes and dream with me

You're home again, what do you see?

You're home again, and there's the sun

Another day has just begun

Do you recall this special day?

I chose it for our dream today

It's someone's birthday once again

She's turning three, the day begins

There's children's laughter, a glow on her face

There's presents around and Mom's cutting the cake

But it's getting dark now, the day's almost done

All of the children are on their way home

Then tomorrow will come and take this away

And leave us the memory of yesterday

Which brings us to now and the end of our dream

And reminds us that time's not as long as it seems

So as you awake and the sun's coming up

Remember tomorrow has never been touched.

CINDY CASH—AGE 19

My third birthday.

My third birthday party. Me at far end; Kathy to my right; my best friend, Christy Wooley (Sheb Wooley's daughter), next to Kathy; and Rosanne at far right.

Kathy and me.

Dad, having a large fan club by now, always wrote, along with Mom, a personal letter to his fans to include in their monthly newsletter, and still does this today.

The following are letters written by them both in 1964.

Dear Club Members,

The year 1964 has been the biggest year yet, so far as our record sales are concerned. Four songs that we recorded received citations of achievement from Broadcast Music, Inc. (BMI)

"UNDERSTAND YOUR MAN", according to two different polls was the biggest song of the year. "RING OF FIRE" was the biggest album of the year.

"Congratulations to my friend, Buck Owen, for being #1 in all the polls, making him Top Country Singer of the Year. He truly deserves it, and never a better man received the honor."

End of bragging.

In the future, our album plans are another album of hymns, (with the Statler Brothers) an album of real old western songs, another album of country ballads, (such as "NOW THERE WAS A SONG") plus single records, of course, and the very best we can produce.

So you can see we're gonna' be busy, especially since the tours will come along too...... so I'd better get on the ball.

Gratefully,

Johnny Cash

Johnny Cash

Dear Club Members,

It seems the past year has flown by, however, a lot has happened in the past twelve months. Johnny is still traveling throughout the world, and feels privileged to meet new friends in every state in the United States.

The children are fast growing up. Rosanne is now in the fourth grade, Kathy is in third, and Cindy has just started her career for the next twelve years. They all three love school and if I might brag a bit, are all doing very well in school. Needless to say, Johnny and I are very proud of our four daughters. Tara is as busy as any curious three year old would be, but life would be very dull without the children to keep one active and on your toes at all times.

To add to my activities, I have just purchased a beauty shop in the town of Oak View, California , about two miles from home. I do not intend to work, but am enjoying the experience and am spending what time I have in the shop.

The children have two horses, "Snuffy" and "Babe", and "Babe" recently foaled, producing a beautiful black and white pinto. As the girls say, "It was a boy". He is having a hard time traveling up and down the mountain on his wobbly legs.

Johnny was home for all the holidays the latter part of the year, and we are looking forward to a big year in 1965, in many ways. Mainly, we pray for the continued good health of our children, for we have certainly been blessed with the good health of our four daughters.

Thanks to each and every one of you for your thoughtfullness in writing, and the wonderful personal things you have sent to us. May everything that is good be yours in 1965. God bless you all.

Sincerely,

Vivian Cash

Vivian Cash

Dad.

Dad.

Dad with the Tennessee Three: Luther Perkins, W. S. "Fluke" Holland, and Marshall Grant. Fluke is still with Dad today.

Dad.

If I Could Rhyme

If I could rhyme

The tick of time

The sound of rain

The who of sane

The fear of death

The good of breath

The maybe of guess

The cry of confess

The hate of fight

The peace of right

The creep of blight

The speed of light

That laugh at night

And then if I could comprehend

The good of men

The bad of men

And who should win

And what is sin

The shock of cold

The good of gold

Respect of old

What grip to hold

Of all I'm told

How long to hold

How strong to hold

How much to hold

Of what I'm told

The pain of dawn

The gone of gone

The limit of gone

The end of friend

The end of end

By math of trend

And the place, time and reason for

The break of bend

The scar of mend

The force of wind

The yield of rend

And understand and accept

The miracle of seed

The cry of need

The good of weed

The total of breed

And not cry for

The salt of song

The short of long

The feel of belong

All day long

I'd tell the world I know it

And I'd be a heck of a poet.

JOHNNY CASH

54

Daddy Will Pick You Up Today

Me.

The mountain in Casitas Springs. Our house is a little more than halfway down but hidden by trees.

The playhouse in the backyard in Casitas Springs that Dad had built for us.

Growing up in such a shadow as Johnny Cash's daughter has at times been overwhelming. These times have been both good and bad. The question I get the most is, "What is it like being Johnny Cash's daughter?" I don't know the answer to that question, because I don't know what it is like to be anyone else's daughter.

The first time it hit me that my father was different from other fathers was when I was in third grade. Dad had been on the road and was going to pick me up from school. I normally rode the bus home. I was excited, not only because I didn't have to ride the bus, but because my friends would get to see that I did, in fact, have a father. That was all I could think about during school. I felt like my friends didn't even believe I had a father because he was never involved in our school activities.

Finally, school was dismissed and I went outside to wait. My friends all gathered around me and I was so proud. Dad drove up in our black Cadillac and his hair was cut short and greased back. He was wearing dark 1950s-style sunglasses and he looked like something out of a James Dean movie.

My heart was pounding with excitement. Then my heart sank and my excitement turned into anger when one of my friends said, "Do you think your daddy will give me his autograph?" They didn't see this man as my father, but as Johnny Cash. I was so confused. I guess that sometimes wishes really do come true, because, at that moment, I wished that my dad would never pick me up at school again. He never did. The next time he came to my school was for my high school graduation.

When I was a kid I used to wish my life was normal. Recently, my friend Linda Freeman told me, "Nothing's normal . . . Normal's what you're used to." She's right.

D ad used to always bring home surprises for us, such as dolls from foreign countries and autographed photos from other celebrities.

I still have some of the autographed photos he brought to me. The Beatles were the most exciting, of course.

Clayton Moore, the Lone Ranger. Inscription reads: "To Cindy, Be a Brave Little Girl, The Lone Ranger."

The Beatles. Inscription reads: "To Cindy and Tara, Love from the Beatles." All four of them signed it.

Rosanne, Kathy, and me. I don't know why I look so scared.

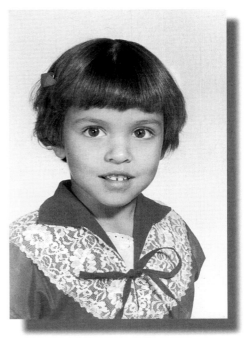

Me, kindergarten, age five.

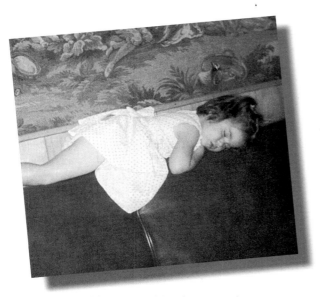

Tara could fall asleep anywhere.

Rosanne, Kathy, me, and Tara.

I still have almost every postcard and letter my dad ever sent to me. He wrote or called every week.

A winter scene in the Badlands. Theo. Roosevelt National Memorial Park. North Dakota—18

Published by North Dakota Scenes, 518 Divide Ave., Bismarck.

POST CARD

Hi Cindy I love you baby. See you in a few days. I love Daddy

Address
Miss Cindy Cash
P.O. Box 44
Casitas Springs,
Calif—

Dad.

My confirmation at age seven. I am in the front row, third from the left.

Dad at home in his office in Casitas Springs.

Dad relaxing at home.

Dad in his office.

Dad and Rosanne.

My dad's oldest brother, Roy Cash
(on left), with Dad.

Dad tuning his guitar.

Mom waiting backstage somewhere on the road.

Dad.

My Parents Divorce

I wrote this story as a high school project in a creative writing class when I was fifteen years old. Our teacher told us to write a short story about something factual that had happened in our life. This was the first thing that came to me.

"Is Daddy coming home for Christmas, Mama?" Tara asked.

"I don't know. We'll just have to wait and see."

It was December 20, a cold, foggy day. Mama was standing in the kitchen cooking breakfast for her four impatient daughters. Only five more days till Christmas and Santa Claus would be here. Rosanne and Kathy were hoping and praying Santa wouldn't forget about the bicycles they wanted so much. Cindy was thinking hard about the bright, shiny red wagon she had asked Santa for in every store she'd seen him in. Tara really didn't care what he brought her. She'd be happy with any toy.

Cindy sat at the window listening closely to every sound she heard, hoping one of them would be the sound of her daddy's car coming up their long driveway. He just had to get home before Christmas Day. It wouldn't be the same without Daddy leading his family into the front room Christmas morning where Santa had been the night before. It was the most exciting day of the year.

Daddy was away from home often. He worked on the road traveling from town to town. Whenever he returned home, he always seemed so tired and restless.

The days went by and Christmas Eve soon arrived. What a beautiful morning. It was too bad it never snowed in Casitas Springs, California, but the foggy day still gave the small town the Christmas spirit.

Hours went by; still no Daddy. The four girls sat by their Christmas tree in the front room rattling the ornately wrapped gifts.

"I wonder what this is."

"I don't know. Mama bought it for Daddy."

"I wish Daddy would hurry. He has to be in bed before Santa Claus comes."

Mama walked in and sat down by her children. She didn't look too happy. It was probably because Daddy wasn't home

yet. She worried about him whenever he was late arriving, if he did come home. For years Daddy was following the same routine: home for a week or so at a time, then gone for two weeks or so at a time.

Then the back door slammed. The girls jumped up and ran to the door. It was Daddy! He hugged his four happy daughters. He really missed them. But where was Mama? Daddy walked back to his bedroom after being smothered with hugs and kisses by his children. Mama and Daddy were in the bedroom for a long time.

Finally Mama came out and told her children to hurry and get in bed because Santa would be there soon. Daddy came out and kissed them good night. Mama wasn't smiling like she should have been.

It was a restless night for everyone. The kids couldn't sleep because of the excitement that would surround them the next morning. They could hear their mama and daddy talking most of the night. There were some words in their conversation that were kind of difficult to understand for the girls.

Morning finally arrived, but only Mama led her children to the front room.

"Oh! Look at all the presents."

"Where's Daddy, Mama?"

"He's very tired. He doesn't feel too well. He's going to sleep now but he'll be out later."

Rosanne and Kathy got their wish and were already outside riding their bicycles. Cindy was sitting in her new red wagon opening her last presents. And Tara couldn't pull herself away from all her goodies.

Cindy had heard her mama and daddy talking the night before and she was confused. She went outside to talk to her older sister.

"Rosanne, I heard Mama say last night that everything was final. What's a divorce?"

Through the Eyes of a Child

My mom and dad were divorced when I was nine years old.

I remember it so well.

My mom took each of us girls, one by one, to our rooms to "talk." She started with Rosanne, naturally; everything always seemed to be done "in order of age," even walking into the living room on Christmas morning. First Dad, then Mom, then Rosanne, Kathy, Cindy, and Tara.

This day was definitely not the feeling of Christmas morning. Something was wrong.

She started this talk with, "Cindy, your daddy and I are getting a divorce."

I replied with, "What's a divorce?"

I'll never forget her answer as long as I live.

"Well, you know how Daddy is not here most of the time? The only difference will be that his clothes and all the things in his office will be gone. You will still see him just as much."

I replied with, "Well, as long as I'll still see him, that's okay."

How simple the mind of a child works. My God, if I had only known then how my whole world would turn around, I would have clung to those clothes with all my might.

I found out years later that my mother was advised by a doctor to divorce my father or she would die and someone else would be raising her children. She was down to ninety pounds and smoking four packs of cigarettes a day. That was all she needed to hear: "Someone else will be raising your children."

She filed for divorce and had my dad served with the papers while he was on the road in Denver. She never knew when he'd be home. She had also waited for the month of August so we would be out of school and might not have to hear the gossip from schoolmates due to the press. She filed on a Friday and took us away for the weekend with a friend, hoping to keep us busy when it hit the papers. She was horrified that the news wasn't released until Monday, after we returned home. All of her efforts to protect us seemed to be of no use.

The next thing I remember was Dad clearing out his office. I sat on the floor watching him pack his things into boxes. I don't think I felt any real emotions at that moment, because the reality had been numbed by Mom's words, "You'll still see him just as much."

Then he was gone.

Dad Moves to Tennessee

Aerial view of Dad's house on the lake in Hendersonville, Tennessee. I got lost the first time I visited the eighteen thousand square feet of this new part-time home.

After my parents divorced, Dad moved to Nashville. He moved into an apartment with Waylon Jennings. After a few months, he requested that Mom allow us to come for a visit. She would not agree. She didn't feel like an apartment with two bachelors was an appropriate environment for four young girls. Dad was so disappointed, so Waylon persuaded him to go out and buy a house. Then maybe Mom would agree to let us visit him.

Dad purchased a house on Old Hickory Lake in Hendersonville, Tennessee, and Mom agreed to let us go. This was the first time we had ever been separated from Mom, and we were terrified. Dad was somewhat of a stranger to us because of his frequent traveling in the past few years. We were all a little scared and feeling awkward this first visit.

Daddy was leaving

We kissed him goodbye

He'd send for us later

We needn't not cry

Mama assured us

He'd love us forever

But it came to a time

They would not live together

So Daddy, he traveled

In search of a home

But found he was lonely

To live so alone

So we flew through the sky

To a faraway land

And walked through the door

Of his home, hand in hand

Oh, what a place

Could this really be home?

There was always just one

That I'd ever known

Is he glad that we're here?

He's so quiet and still

I don't know what to say

Does he know how I feel?

It seems like so long

Since I've seen him at all

I never realized

He was so tall

We've come face to face

Now it's just him and me

What is he thinking?

Who does he see?

I think I'll just sit here

And leave him alone

He looks like he's troubled

I want to go home

I wish he would talk

So I'd know what to say

Well, maybe we'll talk

Some other day

Maybe next summer

We'll visit again

If only he knew

How I'll miss him till then

CINDY CASH—AGE 18

Our first visit to Dad's house. L to R: me, Kathy,
Rosanne, and Dad, with Tara on his lap.

Mom and Dad Both Remarry

Dad and June.

The second summer we went to Tennessee, Dad had married June Carter and we had a new stepmother and two new stepsisters, Carlene, who was a year younger than Rosanne, and Rosie, who was my age. They all lived with Dad now, and I found it a little difficult to call this place home. They were obviously settled here, and we squeezed in where we could fit.

There were six daughters now, but we all eventually adjusted peacefully.

The same year, my mother married a man named Dick Distin. She is still married to him today and they have a wonderful marriage.

I had a very hard time accepting my stepfather at first. It just didn't feel right to have another man at my mother's side. Today I thank God he is there. Through my teen years, I feel, I was at times unkind to Dick; however, he was never unkind to me.

Mom and Dick's wedding photo.

The following are just a couple of the many letters I still have from Dad. He always wrote to us individually.

London, England
May 11th 1968

Dear Cindy;

Hi Sweets!

I sure do miss you. I'm a long way from home and I'm working hard every night.

It will be about two more weeks before I'll be back to the United States, and I'll call you then.

I'll be out there to see you some time in June, and we'll make plans for you to come back to Tennessee, probably in July. We're going to have a lot of fun this Summer.

I love you baby, and I miss you.

Be sweet.

Love
Daddy

P.S. June said Hi.

HOUSE OF CASH

CAUDILL DRIVE
HENDERSONVILLE,
TENNESSEE 37075

May 24 '69

Dear Cindy;

Goodness gracious, me, oh my
Cindy is a sweetie pie!
Tra La La, and whoop-de-doo
I love you, cross my heart I do.

Love
Daddy

Hendersonville
Feb. 9, 1971

Dear Cindy,

When that old earth began to shake
Miss Cindy Cash was wide awake
It rattled window panes and doors
And topsy-turvy went the floors
It made a noise just like a bomb
And Cindy crawled in bed with mom.

I sure am glad you're ok. John Carter knows your
name now. I showed him your picture today and he
said, "Tin-dy."

Write me. I love you.

Daddy

"IT'S A BOY AND HIS NAME AIN'T SUE!"

That's what the headlines read in almost every newspaper across the country when my brother was born March 3, 1970, to Dad and June.

I was in the fifth grade and I remember my principal, Sister Josephine, calling me out of class to take a phone call from my mother giving me the news. I was really excited but feeling a little left out. After all, I had a new brother but he was two thousand miles away in Tennessee. When I finally did get to see him, I fell in love with him, and with the thought of having a brother.

My Half Brother

Dad holding John Carter Cash,
my new brother.

Grandpa Cash (holding Jethro),
John Carter, and Grandma Cash.

68

John Carter Cash, Arrives March 3, 1970

Dad and John Carter on "Hee Haw," 1975.

John Carter

Exchanging smiles we understand

We've shared a special home

And no one else can live within

The world that we have known

There's many things I'd like to say

But somehow you can tell

That in my heart you hold a place

That no one else can fill

CINDY CASH—AGE 26

John Carter—his first birthday.

Church

My mother is a devout Catholic and raised my sisters and me in Catholicism. We were all baptized in church as babies, had our first communion at age seven, and went to confession and wore uniforms while attending Catholic school from first grade to high school graduation.

One of the conditions in my parents' divorce agreement was that Dad would take us to Catholic church every Sunday that we were in his care. He tried. I was eleven the first time, but I remember it as if it were yesterday:

I can feel the weight of the stares. Why is everyone looking at us? We go to church every Sunday with Mom and no one stares at us. Is something wrong with Dad?

This is the first time I ever remember being in church without my mom. It feels very strange. I know I'm supposed to be here. It's Sunday. Mom says you never miss church unless you're very sick. Still, Dad doesn't seem to be at ease at all. He doesn't know when to kneel, sit, or stand. He's watching everyone else, including my sisters and me, to see what to do next.

The priest is praying and all heads are bowed. I know I'm supposed to be very quiet or I go straight to my room when I get home. But wait. Home is far away this Sunday. Mom is far away. My room tonight is at a hotel with Dad.

Before I can make anything out of this whole experience, Dad whispers for us to come on; we're leaving. But the priest has just started talking.

We're now outside the church and people are taking our pictures. We're walking to a long black limousine and the doors close with us inside. Part of me is relieved. The other part of me feels I'm doing something wrong. Mom has never left church before it was over.

It's just the five of us now in the back of the limousine. Dad is telling us that we had to leave because we were distracting the others, who were in church for a reason. We had to leave for everyone else's benefit.

What would Mom say?

Dad just said, finally, "I tried."

THE MILWAUKEE JOURNAL
Green Sheet
Saturday, June 20, 1970

—NANA Photo

On a recent visit to California, Johnny Cash took his four daughters by his first wife to the St. Anastasia Roman Catholic Church in Inglewood. Cash is not Catholic but his daughters are. The Cash family had to leave the church after 15 minutes because the young churchgoers got too excited. The daughters are, from left, Kathleen, 13, Tara, 8, Roseanna, 15, and Cindy, 11.

This is another first memory of trying to absorb Dad's fame. It was truly unbelievable to me. Everywhere we went, every person recognized Dad instantly. Everyone in the world knew who he was. Everyone except me.

Dick's children at this time: Tracy, Brandy, and Todd.

Our new stepsisters, Carlene Smith and Rosie Nix (June's daughters from two previous marriages).

In 1968, Dad had his own TV program on ABC, "The Johnny Cash Show." It aired every Wednesday night and was the number one show in the United States the first year it was on.

I remember sitting with Rosanne, Kathy, and Tara at eight o'clock each week waiting to see Dad's show. Every once in a while he would end his show by saying, "Good night to my four little girls in California. Good night, Rosanne, Kathy, Cindy, and Tara. I love you."

It would thrill us to hear him say that. Mom would always let us know when the show was about to start. She knew how we looked forward to it and was totally supportive.

"The Johnny Cash Show."

"The Johnny Cash Show."

72

Various Photos and Writings—1970s

Mom and Dick, my step-father, had bought a house in Ventura, eleven miles from Casitas Springs, overlooking the Pacific Ocean. They still live there today.

Dad standing in front of his house on Old Hickory Lake, Hendersonville, in the wintertime.

At home at Mom's in Ventura, California. Rosanne, Kathy, Tara (sitting in chair), and me (on the floor). About this time, with Dad's overwhelming fame, we received kidnapping threats and had FBI agents placed at our house and were not able to leave until the person was caught. This was an incredibly scary, confusing, and traumatic period for us.

Living with Mom, we attended school in California and every summer, without fail, we flew to Tennessee. We spent at least two to three weeks there, usually in July. If we happened to be there on my birthday, Dad and June always threw a party for me. I shared this party with Rosie, my new stepsister, because we were only sixteen days apart in age. Her birthday is July 13, and mine is July 29.

Our sixteenth birthday was celebrated on the road while Dad was performing in Lake Tahoe, Nevada. We were staying at a house on the lake that was referred to as the Entertainer's House. Whoever was performing at the Sahara Tahoe stayed there. It was great. They supplied us with a full-time gourmet chef and housekeepers. John Carter loved to catch crawdads in traps and then bring them to the chef to prepare.

For our birthday, Rosie and I decided to take the raft out into Lake Tahoe and, not realizing how big it was, after two or three hours, we were lost. Dad had to send a rescue boat to find us. When we returned, they had a wonderful surprise party waiting for us. All of the band members and my family members were present, along with Carl Perkins, who was touring with Dad at the time.

Carl Perkins's gift to me was a poem he wrote. I have always cherished it.

Sweet Sixteen

Sweet sixteen, a time in life, when living really begins

Ladyhood is on its way and the childlife starts to end

Today the world belongs to you, your beauty, charm and love

And as the tomorrows come and go

You'll find love comes from above

Last night, I heard you say

What a great Dad you have

Realizing this at sweet sixteen

You already know what love is about

So keep that smile, sweet Cindy

Share your love with the world

There's really nothing that can keep you

From being a happy girl

Remember, we usually get back from life

Mostly what we put in

Tomorrow's just around the corner, Cindy

But today it all begins

I've loved you since you were a babe

I've watched you grow with time

Happy Birthday, Cindy, my love

You'll always be a dear friend of mine

CARL PERKINS—1974

In Lake Tahoe, Nevada, watching
Dad's performance. L to R: Me, Rosie, Tara, and Carlene.

Me and Carl Perkins.

Rosanne, Kathy, and me as teenagers.

Dad and me, 1978.

Dad wrote this song in 1970. When I was a teenager, it always made me proud whenever I'd hear him sing it. Maybe the fact that he had six teenage girls in his life was the inspiration for it.

What Is Truth?

The old man turns off the radio

Says: "Where did all the old songs go?

Kids sure play funny music these days!

And they play it in the strangest ways

Everything seems so loud and wild

It was peaceful back when I was a child."

Well, man, could it be the girls and boys

Are trying to be heard above your noise?

And the lonely voice of youth cries:

"WHAT IS TRUTH?"

A little boy of three sittin' on the floor

Looks up and says, "Daddy, what is war?"

"Son, that's when people fight and die!"

The little boy of three says, "Daddy, why?"

And the lonely voice of youth cries:

"WHAT IS TRUTH?"

A young man of seventeen in Sunday school

Is being taught the golden rule

By the time another year's gone around

He may have to lay his own life down!

Can you blame the voice of youth for asking:

"WHAT IS TRUTH?"

A young man sittin' on the witness stand

The man with the book says, "Raise your hand!

Repeat after me, I solemnly swear"

The judge looks down at his long hair

And although the young man solemnly swore

Nobody wanted to hear anymore

And it really didn't matter if the truth was there

It was the cut of his clothes and the length of his

hair

And the lonely voice of youth cries:

"WHAT IS TRUTH?"

The Vietnam War severely affected the whole world. This was Dad's interpretation of his feelings at the time. It was also his attempt to answer the constant question "Why do you always wear black?"

Man in Black

You wonder why I always dress in black

Why you never see bright colors on my back

And why does my appearance always have a somber tone

Well, there's a reason for the things that I have on

I wear the black for the poor and beaten down

Living in the hopeless, hungry side of town

I wear it for the prisoner who has long paid for his crime

That is there because he's a victim of the times

I wear the black for those who've never read

Or listened to the words that Jesus said

About the road to happiness through love and charity

You'd think he's talking straight to you and me

Well, we're doing mighty fine I do suppose

In our streak-o-lightning cars and fancy clothes

But just so we're reminded of the ones who are held back

Up front there ought to be a *man in black*

I wear it for the sick and lonely old

For the reckless ones whose bad trips left them cold

I wear the black in mourning for the lives that could

    have been

Each week we lost a hundred fine young men

I wear it for the thousands who have died

Believing that the Lord was on our side

I wear it for another hundred thousand who have died

Believing that we all were on their side

There are things that never will be right, I know

And things need changing everywhere you go

But till we start to make a move to make a few things right

You'll never see me wear a suit of white

I'd love to wear a rainbow every day

To tell the world that everything's o.k.

But I will carry off a little darkness on my back

Until things are brighter, I'm the *man in black*.

I Will Rock and Roll with You

They used to call me rockabilly

All of us ran through

When Elvis opened up the door

Be-bop-a-lop-bam-boo

I didn't ever play much rock and roll

'Cause I got so much country in my soul

But I'm a different man for lovin' you

And I'd take a shot at what you asked me to

And baby, I will rock and roll with you, if I have to

Memphis, 1955, on Union Avenue

Carl and Jerry and Charlie and Roy

And Billy Riley, too

A new sun risin' on the way we sing

And a world of weirdos waitin' in the wings

But I love you and though I'm past forty-two

There are still a few things yet I didn't do

And baby, I will rock and roll with you, if I have to

Dad took this photo of us the night he was presented with his star on Hollywood Boulevard. I remember how proud I felt that night, and I returned to Hollywood (I was living only sixty miles away with Mom at the time) many times just to look at it and show it to my friends.

My First Marriage and the Birth of My Daughter

Tara and me looking at photos when I lived in the condo in Ventura, shortly after my divorce from Cris.

Do I?

My first love was my high school sweetheart, Cris Brock. Actually, he was the first everything for the young girl I was. We were the class couple and vowed to be husband and wife someday. Well, that day came a little sooner than we'd planned.

Thank God my mother liked Cris. When we broke the news that we were going to have a baby, she was not thrilled, but she immediately started setting our wedding date. I had graduated from high school a few months earlier, but Cris was still a senior. The most terrifying thing I remember her saying was "You need to call your father."

We set our wedding date, a Catholic wedding, but no one was to be told about the baby.

It took me three days to get up enough nerve to call Dad. Our conversation went like this:

Cindy: "Dad, what are you doing January fourteenth?"
Dad: "How far along are you?"

I was speechless, but finally answered.
Cindy: "Six weeks."
Dad: "I'll be there."

I hung up the phone and stood there a minute thinking, "What in the world just happened? How did he know?" I sure wasn't going to call back and inquire. It was relief enough to me that the conversation was over.

I got married on January 14, 1977, in a Catholic church, with all the rituals intact. I requested that my dad and my mother walk me down the aisle and give me away together. I felt my mother deserved the right to give me away just as much as my father.

On July 22, 1977, I gave birth to my one and only child, my daughter, Jessica Dorraine Brock, who weighed six pounds and twelve ounces. She was my angel and I was terrified. The thought of being responsible for this tiny life at eighteen years old made me numb. Still, I cherished her. I never knew you could love anything so much that it was frightening. She consumed my every thought and every breath.

Cris was totally consumed with fatherhood. He couldn't even fathom the love he felt for Jessica. He worshiped her. He was very good to both of us. However, we were very young and I began to feel like we were growing into two very different people. Maybe I was just getting restless, but I started having anxiety attacks that eventually sent me to a therapist.

I filed for divorce after a year and a half of marriage and moved into a condo with Jessica. I still feel sad when I remember the pain I believe I brought to Cris.

My Move to Tennessee

Jackson (Carlene's son) and Jessica. I took this photo while practicing using a new Nikon camera Dad had given me for my birthday.

Jessica.

Jessica at Rosanne and Rodney's wedding reception, 1979.

Jessica.

My favorite of all the photos I ever shot
of Jessica, taken at the park one day shortly after
our move to Tennessee.

Jessica at our condo in Ventura.

I Do?

Shortly after my divorce from Cris, Dad asked me if I would move to Tennessee for a year. His exact words were "It's my turn to spend some time with you." I was nineteen years old with a baby. He sent the Peterbilt truck that he used on the road, and all my things, including my car, were loaded in his truck and I flew with Jessica to Tennessee. I got an apartment two miles from Dad's house. He had picked it out for me himself before I ever left California.

A few months after moving, I flew Jessica back to California for a visit with my mother and Cris, who both lived in Ventura. When I returned to Tennessee, I got very sick with the flu and went to stay at Dad's house.

One morning, Dad had to leave the house at 4:00 A.M. to do "The Ralph Emery Morning Show." He had told me that he had a new guitar player that he'd like for me to meet and that he was going to be there any minute to pick him up. I had been up sick for most of the night, so I was awake. Dad said he would introduce us when they got home from the TV taping. I was hoping I'd feel better after I showered and dressed. Around ten, Dad came home and called me from my room. "Cindy, this is my new guitar player, Marty Stuart. Stuart, this is my daughter, Cindy."

Sparks were flying already.

There was something about this man I wanted to know better, and I sensed he felt the same way.

That weekend, Dad asked me to go along on the bus to Virginia to play the Carter Fold, June's old homeplace where a lot of her family put on weekend shows and where Dad and June visited and joined the show about once a year.

I think Marty and I fell in love over biscuits at June's aunt Fern's house. We were together for the next eight years. We became inseparable. I joined Dad's road show full-time. Dad would introduce me as his "biggest hit from 1958, my daughter, Cindy Cash."

Marty and I had a lot of fun and Dad and I became the closest of friends. After twenty-one years, I finally got to know him as a person, a father, and a friend. These next few years were priceless to me.

Marty and I were married two years later, on March 31, 1983. We decided to marry on Friday since Saturday, the traditional Christian wedding day, fell on April Fools' Day.

Dad and June were in the Bahamas. They had just finished a long tour and desperately needed solitude and rest. I still have the beautiful letter he wrote me apologizing for not being able to attend our wedding.

We had never set a date, so it was a spur-of-the-moment decision. I had two weeks to plan. My mom and stepdad, living in California, were also unable to attend because of prior commitments.

I asked Armando Bisceglia, our head security guard since I was ten years old, to give me away. He drove me to my wedding in Dad's Rolls-Royce wearing his chauffeur's cap. He was very special to me. There were only about twenty people at our wedding. Marty wanted to keep it small, and I was fine with that. My sister Tara was my maid of honor, and Jack "Cowboy" Clement was Marty's best man.

We were married at the First Baptist Church, where Marty was a member, in Smyrna, Tennessee (about twenty miles outside of Nashville).

We didn't have a honeymoon, because five days after we were married Marty had to be in Los Angeles to play guitar on a Bob Dylan recording session.

We were very happy. My daughter was four years old and, immediately after the ceremony, she went up to Marty and said, "Can I call you Daddy now?" Marty cried and became Daddy instantly. Before long they were best of friends. He was so taken with her. She was quite a little girl. She thoroughly entertained Marty. He wrote songs with her and took her all kinds of places. He absolutely loved Christmastime. He'd dress as Santa even after she was asleep. She adored him. He sent her letters and postcards from the road whenever he left town. He was so involved with her life, and took a special interest in Halloween, school plays, and piano practice. He went to her school often and sang songs to her classmates.

Then suddenly, after we'd been together eight years, he was gone. We had an argument one night. Marty hadn't been himself for about a year. He had signed a recording contract with CBS and he'd changed into someone I didn't know anymore. He was distant and unhappy all the time. After this argument, we both left the house; I went to my dad's and he went to his mom's. The next day I came home in the late afternoon and all of his things were gone. Three days later he called and said he wasn't coming home—ever.

I was absolutely devastated. Jessica was almost ten years old and couldn't absorb any of this. I moved in with my dad, and three months later got an apartment for Jessica and me. I lost thirty pounds and began looking anorexic. Within six months, I was close to death. I became completely dependent on prescription painkillers and never ate. After a year of this, my family did an intervention at my home and I entered a treatment center. I was literally dying. I had lost the best friend I'd ever had and now I felt hopeless. The word "divorce" had never been spoken in our house, and, after a year and a half of separation, it still hadn't been discussed.

Sixteen months later, Marty showed up in my life again. He wanted to save the marriage and did not want a divorce. I was very angry. He had totally abandoned me for so long and now he wanted to come home. In my anger, I filed for divorce.

It became final six months later.

Marty and I have been divorced since 1988 and we speak only occasionally. He attended Jessica's high school graduation in June of 1995 (as did her father, Cris) but rarely calls her. She refers to him now as Marty, not Daddy.

For Jessica and me, it's simply impossible to hold on to someone who is gone.

Marty and Jessica.

Marty, Jack
"Cowboy" Clement,
and me on our
wedding day.

Me, Marty, and
Jessica, 1985.

Me and Jessica. She was four years old and
a little ham. She always entertained me and had a
great sense of humor.

Me sitting on Dad's Rolls-Royce, in which
Armando Bisceglia drove me to my wedding.

Love Has Lost Again

I've seen the dark, I've felt the cold

It's time to walk away

Can't take the blame for what you've done

We've played some games nobody won

And now it's time to pay

Love is cruel they always say

And I don't feel so nice

All we seem to do is fight

We grind our teeth and walk so light

I just can't stand the price

There's trouble in my paradise

You're accusing me of lies

And that's just not so

I'm sorry once again, my love

And I've said I'm sorry way too much

Love has lost again

The tears are gone, the nights are long

I've given all I have

I understand the pain you hold

It hurts to feel your heart so cold

Will it ever pass

I can't give you what you want

It's my turn to be free

You've left a hole inside my heart

I know that I have done my part

Good-bye, my love, good-bye

The day Marty and I split, I had just returned home from Cuba. I had gone with Dad, June, John Carter, Carlene, Rosie, and my nephew Thomas (Kathy's son) to perform a concert for American military personnel stationed in Guantánamo Bay.

As we flew home on the U.S. naval plane, I knew in my heart and in my head that Marty was already gone in spirit. It could not become a reality until he actually moved out, but somehow in my gut I knew he was leaving.

Marty and I had agreed that I should go with Dad so we could have a few days apart to see if we could resolve this unknown conflict in our marriage. When I returned home, my marriage was over. I wrote this song on the plane coming home.

There's trouble in my paradise

And you're accusing me of lies

And that's just not so

I'm sorry once again, my love

And I've said I'm sorry way too much

Love has lost again

Oh, love has lost again

Armando, who gave me away in Dad's place.

AUTHOR'S NOTE: After twenty-seven years with the family, Armando passed away two months before I finished writing this book. I am proud that I knew and loved him. I was by his bedside when he died and will always remember him fondly. His wife, Anna, still works for Dad and June, and I have much appreciation for their loyalty to my family over the years.

One of the most memorable and musically educational times of my life was from 1980 to 1983, when I was a regular part of "The Johnny Cash Show." I also went on every tour with my dad and had my own small part of the concert. We would usually sing a duet together and then he'd step in with the band and play guitar while I sang something alone like "Love Me Tender" or "City of New Orleans" or "Blue Suede Shoes" or a song I wrote. After my song, we'd laugh and talk to each other for the audience's benefit, and he always made me feel like I was important and that he was glad I was there. I hope he knew how happy I was to be there.

I learned so much about how to treat an audience and how to always act professional even if I was scared to death. After the show, he'd tell me how good I sang, even if I'd stunk.

These were the years that brought him and me together as friends for the first time in my life. This is when I realized I didn't have to be afraid of him and he didn't have to be afraid of me. I'd finally, for the most part, put the pain of the past to rest. He was no longer the tall, dark, mysterious stranger I had always feared and kept quiet around as a teenager. He was just a man who had felt as awkward around me as I had around him. We had come to understand that we needed each other. We had finally established some kind of relationship between us, and for that I am truly grateful.

On the Road with Dad

Me and Dad on stage, November 1, 1980.

86

Michigan, on stage, 1979.

Me on stage in Canada
in 1989 when I was
singing with the Next
Generation.

Me and Dad.

Germany, on stage with Dad, 1981.

My Eighteenth-Birthday Present from Dad

Cindy, I Love You

We never really got right down to talkin'

We couldn't seem to find the place or time

Distance and the miles between us made us kind of strangers.

And it added to the distance already there between our minds.

And Cindy, I love you, yes I love you, yes I love you

And when I can't think of anything to say

Don't be reading something in my mind that isn't there

Remember, Cindy, I love you anyway.

I look at you and wonder what you're thinking

I'm sure you felt the same a time or two

We must both remember that true love should cost us nothing

You just owe me your affection and I owe the same to you.

And Cindy, I love you, yes I love you, yes I love you

And when I can't think of anything to say

Don't be reading something in my mind that isn't there

Remember, Cindy, I love you anyway

Remember, Cindy, I love you anyway.

Dad was taping "The Merv Griffin Show," and since it was taped in Los Angeles we were with him, as we always were whenever he was in California.

I was turning eighteen the next day, and Dad asked me what I wanted for my birthday. I told him I'd like for him to just write me a poem or something.

He left the room and twenty minutes later he returned.

"Cindy, would you like to hear your birthday present?"

Rosie, Tara, and I were sitting there, and he began to sing.

We all began to cry as he sang "Cindy, I Love You."

Dad recorded this song on the album titled "The Last Gunfighter Ballad" in 1978.

Kathy

Kathy, take that frown from off your face

Let a self-assured expression take its place

For I love you, yes, I love you, yes I do

And you shouldn't let tomorrow bother you

Just rest assured that everything's all right

Then lay you down in sweet, sweet dreams tonight

Kathy, are you listening, did you hear

I love you not a day and not a year

Ah, forever is the timeless time I mean

And I'll prove it to you if you haven't seen

You will know it by the years as they go by

That I'll love you, Kathy, till the day I die

Kathy, be prepared to understand

I'm just a man and nothing but a man

And sometimes I might forget to let you know

But you must always remember that it's so

There's no way that my heart can change for you

I love you, Kathy, don't forget I do

Poems for Our Parents

Mom

I grew up believing that you wrote the book

On being a mother and all that it took

Growing up in a world where the world had our names

Our everyday life followed Daddy's found fame

As part of a family called "wealthy do well"

Still protected by you set my heart out full sail

For you taught me of humble and how it would pay

If I lived by the book staying set in my ways

As nights followed mornings and days became years

The world was my playground, I became your career

You'll never know that when you cried

I was hurt the most but I'd run and hide

Those were the times that I found the word fear

And asked myself then what if you were not here

For if the world crumbled and came to an end

Come hell or high water, I'd still have a friend

Then I'd sit and I'd cry for the rest of the world

Knowing they were deprived, not being one of your girls

But those who have found you, and call you their friend

Have found one that's special to keep to the end

For love's locked in your heart with no key for release

And just knowing you're there is a rare kind of peace

You'll be the one person I'll depend on forever

Your heart made of gold will be my one treasure

And as life hits me harder, it's all I can do

To remember the times I could hold on to you

You defined the word lady and touched it with class

Making sure as my mother I was first, never last

Now, as years have robbed my youth, and someone calls

    me Mom, too

I pray to be one just like you

CINDY CASH—AGE 20

Daddy

You're always a gentleman, fragile, yet strong

Mostly a loner in search of a song.

An angel of mercy stands close by your side

She lost count of the times she kept you alive.

Over and over I've prayed for your health

God kept putting your number back on the shelf.

There've been many things still left on His mind

To send through you from Him time to time.

Do you question the past? Are your memories real?

I know it's hard for you to say how you feel.

You know my love holds no conditions, no price.

In your house made of glass, quiet cuts like a knife.

I know that you love me whenever you can

There is only so much to be asked of one man.

Comfort is seldom and friends come and go

Just look to the ones you truly know.

I remember when it hurt just to think of you

I've come so far now, there's peace that's brand new

Now true love is grounded between you and me

You're always my friend and my heart is set free.

The love that we share is gentle and kind.

It's forgiving and growing while healing with time.

CINDY CASH—AGE 29

An Angel on Earth

Mother, you're an angel on earth

The greatest thing that's ever happened to me.

Ever since the day of my birth

You've had the strength to put up with me.

Out of all of the times I've talked back to you

And made you so mad that you cried,

And all of the heartaches that I've put you through,

After, I'd regret it inside.

Well, I didn't understand how it made you feel

But now that I'm older, I do.

And now that I know all your heartaches were real,

I feel them inside of me, too.

I love you, Mom

You're an angel on earth.

TARA CASH—AGE 15
NOVEMBER 4, 1976

To Dick

You knew that you loved her
As you walked down the aisle
And when she said "I do"
You returned her a smile
You called her your wife
And accepted four daughters
Who were lost in a world
To find you their stepfather
In our lives there would only
Be one man in our home
And the one before you
Had to leave us alone

We rebelled all your love
But you never walked out
And the love in your heart
Never once spoke a doubt
You showed us that love
Was stronger than fear
And that ours would soon pass
As time dried our tears
You never lost hope
You never complained
Even when we'd neglect you
You never showed pain
You loved us as though
We were yours all along

There was never a time
That you didn't belong
As the years slowly passed
We learned to rely
On your strong, settled way
And we knew we'd get by
Your moments of silence
Were a lesson to learn
That to battle within me
Found nothing was earned
You respected me always
When others would burn me

I stood tall in your eyes
You knew not how to harm me
When the world shut me out
And I couldn't be heard
I'd find myself searching
For that peace in your words
You are one I am proud of
To call as my own
You made our lives full
You completed our home.

CINDY CASH—AGE 20

93

John Carter also performed on Dad's show and still does today.

John Carter Cash.

June

I thank you for the many years

You came along to dry my tears

I thank you for your patient ways

I'm thankful when we kneel to pray

I thank you for the laughs we've shared

And thank you, June, for being there.

CINDY CASH—AGE 23

June and me.

$\mathcal{V}$arious Family Photos

Rosanne and me, 1980.

Rosie, Kathy, me, and June, 1980.

Here we are again.

95

Me and Rosie.

Me and Carlene about to go on stage and join Dad at one of his concerts. That night, Stephen King came to the show and got on stage and played the electric guitar. I was very impressed at how well he played and was thrilled to meet him. He had just finished writing the book *Misery* and gave us all a copy. He inscribed in mine: "To Cindy, from your number one fan, Stephen King." I was so flattered because I thought he simply enjoyed the songs I sang on the show. Later, when I went to see the movie, I realized I was obviously mistaken and got a big kick out of it. Then I wondered if he was going to hold me captive like Kathy Bates did to James Caan. Seriously, though, he was a very kind man and a gentleman, and I was proud to have his book and to have met him.

Stephen King and me backstage.

Me and Rosanne in
Jamaica around 1981.

Dad and June.

Dad and Rosanne.

Dad and me.

Tara in 1976. Dad took this photo when he first started getting interested in photography as a hobby. It was taken on a balcony of a hotel in Ventura during one of his visits to see us.

Kathy.

Dad turning the table on a fan taking
a photo of him in Europe.

Mom and Dick, 1989.

Grandparents

To Our Grandparents

Another year has come and gone

You're growing old and time drags on

It seems there's nowhere left to go

You're weaker now, you're moving slow

Memories are close at hand

Reminding you just where you stand

You gave us life, you built our home

So now be sure, you're not alone

For all your children and theirs as well

Remember that you have never failed

To be the ones who paved the way

Our family tree will grow each day

So just sit back, kick off your shoes

And rest assured, we'll follow through

For everything you've worked to be

Lies now within your family

CINDY CASH—AGE 23

"I Remember Mama, 1904—1991"

(WRITTEN FOR GRANDMA CASH)

Carrie Cloveree Rivers Cash (my paternal grandmother). What a great name and is this ever a classic photo. I love to sit and look at every detail of this picture. She was nine years old.

Grandma Cash. I was very close to her and miss her daily. She died on March 11, 1991.

"Mama taught me to be thrifty in finance. She was so happy with so little. She was comfortable in inexpensive clothes and such. What money she had she saved for us, instead of using it on herself. She was a truly good steward."

Louise Cash Garrett

Dad and Grandpa Cash. He was quite a man. He died in 1985.

"So many times Mama would say to me, 'Put your trust in the Lord, son,' and she meant it. It was what she lived by, her complete trust in Jesus. It still carries me today. When I have doubts or doubt any of my people, I put my trust in Him just like she said."

Johnny Cash

101

Ray and Carrie Cash, my paternal grandparents.

"She was such a believer! She read and studied her Bible a lot. Every time I asked her a question, she answered it with scripture, and she was right and that helped me."

Reba Cash Hancock

Dad and Grandma Liberto, 1977.

Tom and Irene Liberto, my maternal grandparents. Grandpa Liberto was an amateur magician and worked with the great Blackstone. Grandpa never gave away his secrets. He taught me to play gin rummy when I was nine years old, and I never won a single game.

"So many times Mama would tell me straight out if I was wrong about something. She told the truth even if it hurt. That really has helped me over the years to be honest with myself and to be true to God. She also was just as quick to compliment me for right things I did, and said she was proud of me."

Joanne Cash Yates

"I can still see her in the kitchen making mashed potatoes. I still see her with her Bible that she loved to read and teach others. I still see her playing the piano with a feel that was her very own. I close my eyes and I still feel her love, her honesty, humility, and peace. I also remember that even though she was near death, she never complained about dying, even though she loved life. She was ready to meet our Savior. I still miss her every day."

Tommy Cash

Grandma Liberto, Mom, Aunt Sylvia (Mom's sister), and "Nanny" (my maternal great-grandmother), or Dora. Nanny lived to be ninety-nine.

Clockwise from L to R: Me, Dick, Tara, Grandma Liberto, Mom, and Thomas (Kathy's son).

Dad with his siblings and parents. L to R: Tommy Cash, Roy Cash (died August 23, 1992), Grandpa Cash, Dad, Grandma Cash, Reba Hancock, and Louise Garrett.

Mama's Thoughts

I'm getting old—my step is slow

My eyes are getting dim

But I've read the Word and walk the line

And give my heart to Him

No one can say—I didn't care

Or took the time to pray

I've tried to light my children's path

And do some good each day

Before I go—please remember

God's memories fill my cup

And don't look down on anyone

Except to help them up

I'm not ready—but I'm well prepared

To walk the sunset way

Just remember please—by the will of God

I'll see you all someday . . .

ROY CASH

Papa Cash

Tell me what you know 'bout the Alamo

You graduated school, you told me so

I fought the battle of World War I

A proud American, my country won!

I raise my flag in my front yard

But each passing day, it's getting hard

I'm weaker now, and moving slow

But listen close before you go

I really love the simple life

I've always stood beside my wife

I love it when you all drop in

And ask me how my day has been

I've never been a man of wealth

But, thank you, Lord, I had my health

Yeah, I reckon after all

Looking back, we had it all

Did rich folk thank the Lord each day

Or did they just forget to pray?

Well, I remember many times

How I would work just to make a dime

Still, every night we'd thank the Lord

Yeah, prayer was easy to afford

The less we had, the more we tried

We never had a thing to hide

So how did all those fancy men

Ride trains and have so many friends?

I know there's nothing stopping me

I've lived and worked where men are free

Now the world has changed, it's not the same

And progress turns into a game

Who is right, who is wrong?

Who is weak and who is strong?

But God has never changed his mind

It's man that has left the peace behind

When TV wasn't all we heard

We seemed to lean on Jesus' words

And now, our Bibles left unread

The TV's on, the news is read

The speaker reads the current news

We tremble, are we gonna lose?

Did we forget the days of old

And lose ourselves, afraid and cold

Or is there still a gleam of hope

To pass down wisdom from the older folk?

And pass along the sweet embrace

That held us close to all we faced

CINDY CASH—AGE 22

randma and Grandpa Cash were married sixty-five years when Grandpa died in 1985. Grandma died March 11, 1991. We buried her on her eighty-seventh birthday.

Grandpa raising the flag in his front yard, as he did every single day until he was physically unable to. He was a World War I veteran and so proud of it. He was given a twenty-one-gun salute at his funeral, and he would have been so proud of that.

Ragged Old Flag

By Johnny Cash

I walked through a county courthouse square

On a park bench an old man was sitting there

I said, "Your courthouse is kinda run-down"

He said, "Naw, it'll do for our little town"

I said, "Your flagpole has leaned a little bit

And that's a Ragged Old Flag you got hanging on it"

He said, "Have a seat," and I sat down

"Is this the first time you've been in our little town?"

I said, "I think it is," he said, "I don't like to brag

But we're kinda proud of that Ragged Old Flag

You see, we got a little hole in that flag there

When Washington took it across the Delaware

And it got powder burned the night Francis Scott Key

Sat up watchin' it writing 'Say Can You See'

And it got a little rip in New Orleans

With Pakenham and Jackson tuggin' at its seams

And it almost fell at the Alamo

Beside the Texas flag, but she waved on though

She got cut with a sword at Chancellorsville

And she got cut again at Shiloh Hill

There was Robert E. Lee, Beauregard and Bragg

And the south wind blew hard on that Ragged Old Flag

On Flanders Field in World War I

She got a big hole from a Bertha Gun

She turned blood red in World War II

She hung limp and low by the time it was through

She was in Korea and Vietnam

She went where she was sent by her Uncle Sam

Native Americans, brown, yellow and white

All shed red blood for the Stars and Stripes

In her own good land here she's been abused

She's been burned, dishonored, denied and refused

And the very government for which she stands

Has been scandalized throughout the land

And she's getting threadbare and she's wearing thin

But she's in good shape for the shape she's in

'Cause she's been through the fire before

And I believe she can take a whole lot more

So we raise her up every morning, take her down
        every night

We don't let her touch the ground and fold her up right

On second thought I do like to brag

'Cause I'm mighty proud of that Ragged Old Flag."

Five Feet High and Rising

By Johnny Cash

How high's the water, Mama?

Two feet high and rising

How high's the water, Papa?

She said it's two feet high and rising

But we can make it to the road in a homemade boat

'Cause that's the only thing we got left that'll float

It's already over all the wheat and oats

Two feet high and rising

How high's the water, Mama?

Three feet high and rising

How high's the water, Papa?

She said it's three feet high and rising

Well, the hives are gone, I lost my bees

Chickens are sleepin' in the willow trees

Cows in water up past their knees

Three feet high and rising

How high's the water, Mama?

Four feet high and rising

How high's the water, Papa?

She said it's four feet high and rising

Hey, come look through the window pane

The bus is comin', gonna take us to the train

Looks like we'll be blessed with a little more rain

Four feet high and rising

How high's the water, Mama?

Five feet high and rising

How high's the water, Papa?

She said it's five feet high and rising

Well, the rails are washed out north of town

We gotta head for higher ground

We can't come back till the water goes down

Five feet high and rising

Well, it's five feet high and rising

More Family Photos

Dick and Mom today.

Tara, Kathy, Dad, and me.

L to R: Me, Fred (Tara's husband), Hannah
(Rodney's daughter), John Carter, and Kathy.

Kathy and Mom.

Tara can always make me laugh. She's a special person with a heart of gold.

110

Rosanne, Kathy,
Mom, Tara,
and me.

Dad and Rosanne on stage.

My Old Man

By Rosanne Cash

The old man's laughing tonight

He's young beyond his fears

But then the smile drops from his eyes

And we all wind up in tears

The old man's crying tonight

'Cause it all happened so fast

He's frightened by the future

Embarrassed by the past

So let him be who he wants to be

'Cause he ain't ever gonna be young again

And let him see who he needs to see

'Cause he never had too many friends

And ask him how he remembers me

'Cause I want to know where I stand

How I love my old man

The old man's restless tonight

Just trying to kill his pain

He believes what he says he believes

But that don't make him a saint

The old man's lonesome tonight

And he just wants to go home

All those fools who stand in his way

Why can't they leave him alone

So let him be who he wants to be

'Cause he ain't ever gonna be young again

And let him see who he needs to see

'Cause he never had too many friends

And ask him how he remembers me

'Cause I want to know where I stand

How I love my old man

Rosanne's first publicity photo. It's still one of my favorites.

Ron Keith and me. He's been one of my best friends for over twenty years and took most of the more current photos in this book. He's always been very close to everyone in my family and he's my favorite photographer in the world. Thank you, Ron.

Kathy's family. Clockwise from left: Jimmy (Kathy's husband of fourteen years), Thomas, Kathy, Kacy, and Dustin.

Me and Dad.

Mom's and Dad's Grandchildren

Children

The meaning of truth is found in the minds

Of children at play just biding their time.

They're far behind greed. They've nothing to lose.

Their minds are at peace. They've nothing to prove.

The tears that are shed over broken down toys

Are tears they'll remember as ones to enjoy

They know only simple which makes them so wise

Their love speaks so loudly it never tells lies

So rock-a-bye babies and dream only love

And thank the sweet Lord who's watching above

And take your sweet time to pass that time by

Youth passes quickly and time surely flies

Keep your pace slow and your heart open wide

Holding close to those days when you were a child

CINDY CASH—AGE 21

114

Rosanne's Children

When Rosanne married Rodney Crowell in 1979, he had a daughter, Hannah, from a previous marriage. Rosanne and Rodney were married for thirteen years and together they had three daughters—Caitlin, born in 1980; Chelsea, born in 1982; and Carrie, born in 1988.

The following photos include Rodney and Hannah. Although Rosanne and Rodney were divorced in 1992, Rodney and Hannah remain close to our hearts and we see them often.

Rosanne got married again in 1995, to John Leventhal.

Dad holding Carrie Kathleen Crowell (Rosanne's youngest daughter).

Caitlin Rivers Crowell (Rosanne's oldest daughter).

Caitlin, Thomas,
Jessica, Hannah, and
Chelsea Jane Crowell.

Rodney, Caitlin, Rosanne, and Chelsea when
Rosanne was presented with her star at the Country
Music Hall of Fame in Nashville.

Chelsea and Caitlin, Easter 1986.

Chelsea with Kathy's son Dustin.

Rodney leading (L to R) Hannah, Caitlin, Jessica, and Thomas in search of Easter eggs at Dad's house.

Caitlin, Chelsea, and Hannah (in chair), holding Carrie.

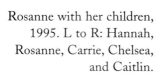

Rosanne with her children, 1995. L to R: Hannah, Rosanne, Carrie, Chelsea, and Caitlin.

$\mathcal{K}$athy's Children

Kathy had one son from an early marriage, Thomas Gabriel Coggins, born in 1973. She has been married to Jimmy Tittle since 1982.

They have two children—James Dustin Tittle, born in 1984, and Kacy Rosanne Tittle, born in 1987.

Mom holding four-year-old Thomas.

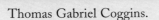

Thomas Gabriel Coggins.

Thomas, 1984.

Kacy Rosanne and James Dustin Tittle, 1989.

Dad holding Dustin, 1989.
I love this photo. Dad is truly
loving being a granddad.

Dustin and Kacy when she was eight weeks old. Dad took this photo.

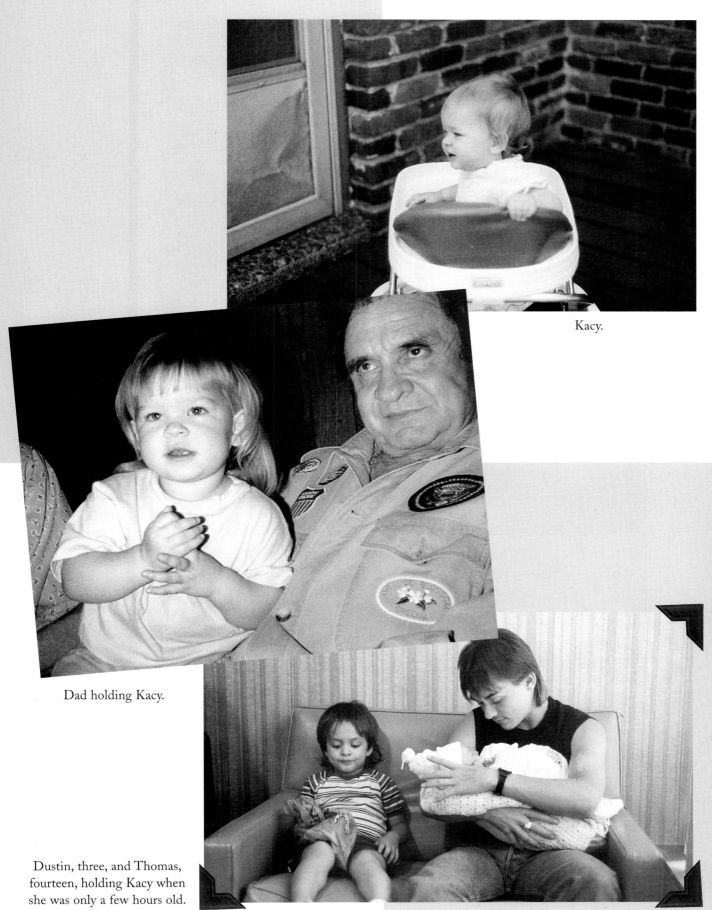

Kacy.

Dad holding Kacy.

Dustin, three, and Thomas, fourteen, holding Kacy when she was only a few hours old.

121

Thomas holding Dustin and Kacy.

Me and Thomas dancing at his eighteenth birthday party. Mom and Dick flew in from California to Tennessee to surprise him.

Jessica, Cindy's Daughter, Arrives July 22, 1977

Jessica Dorraine Brock with Thomas, 1977.

Dad holding Jessica.

John Carter and Jessica.

Jessica's third-grade picture.

Mom holding Jessica.

Hannah and Jessica.

Dad did many television specials and included the grandchildren occasionally.

This photo of Jessica was taken during a rehearsal for a Christmas special at the Grand Ole Opry on October 3, 1985. She was extremely bored.

Jessica.

Jessica catching crawdads in the creekbed.

Jessica, age four.

Me and Jessica.

Jessica was Strawberry Shortcake for Halloween (age six).

Me and Dad with Jessica on his knee, 1988, at an auction at her school. Dad donated a guitar to the cause.

Aran, Tara's Son, Arrives November 21, 1994

Tara married Fred Schwoebel in 1991. They have one son, Aran Thomas Schwoebel. He was born on November 21, 1994.

Fred, Tara, and Aran, 1994.

Fred and Aran sleeping.

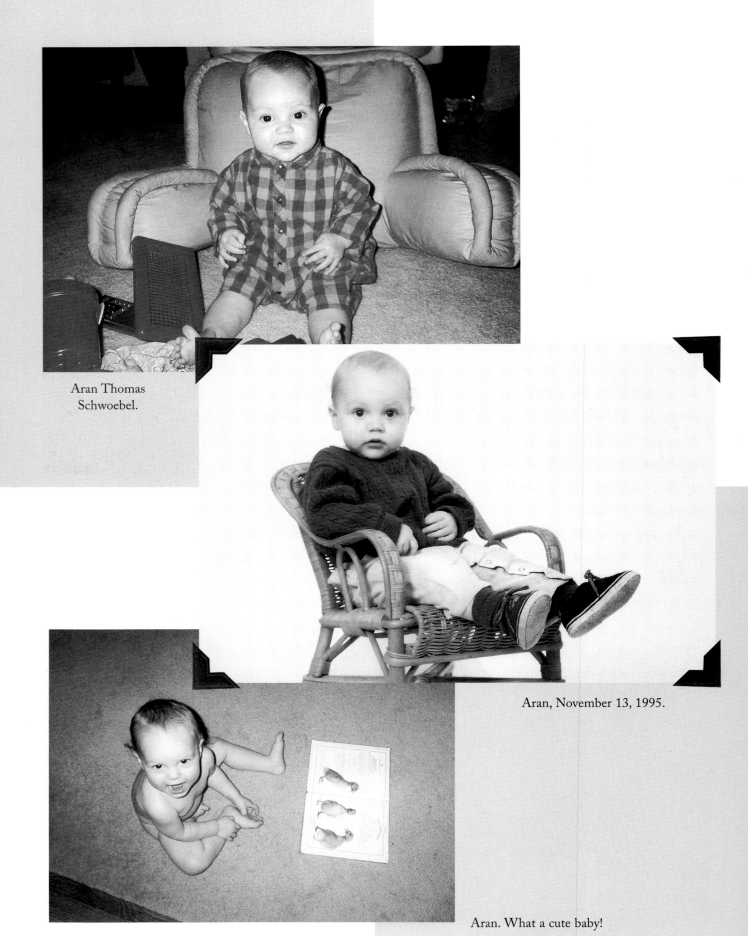

Aran Thomas
Schwoebel.

Aran, November 13, 1995.

Aran. What a cute baby!

128

Joseph, John Carter's Son, Arrives February 25, 1996

John Carter married Mary Joska on June 14, 1995, so I now have a sister-in-law. She's one of the most loving, kind, and spiritual people I've ever known. I truly love her, and she has made John Carter very happy.

They went to Israel for their honeymoon, and three weeks after they returned we got the news that Mary was pregnant.

The newest addition to our family is Joseph John Cash, who was born on February 25, 1996, and is beautiful.

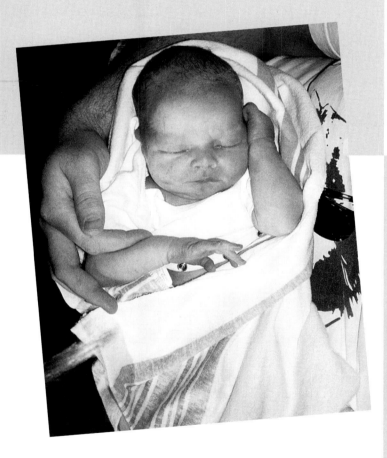

Joseph John Cash (one day old), born one day before Dad's sixty-fourth birthday.

John Carter and Mary Cash.

My stepdad, Dick, has three children from a previous marriage. So in addition to Carlene and Rosie, I acquired two stepbrothers and one more stepsister later that same year, when Mom married Dick. Dick's children are Tracy Distin, who was born in 1961; Brandy Distin Anderson, who was born in 1964; and Todd Distin, who was born in 1967.

My Stepbrothers and

Tracy Distin and his son, Sean.

Todd Distin.

Todd, Tracy, Brandy, Christopher Anderson (Brandy's husband), Sean, and Amber and Crystal (Brandy and Christopher's daughters).

130

Stepsisters and Their Children

Carlene has two children: Tiffany Simpkins Lowe, who was born in 1973, and John Jackson Routh, who was born in 1976.

Carlene (June's daughter) and me. Her son, Jackson, is sitting at the table with a biscuit in his mouth, being a ham for the camera. Ron Keith is beside me with his back to the camera.

Tiffany holding Jessica on her shoulders.

Tiffany Simpkins Lowe. I call her Tiffer.

John Jackson Routh, age four.

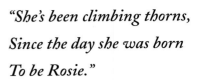

"She's been climbing thorns,
Since the day she was born
To be Rosie."
Jeff Williams, aka J. W. Younger
Donny Meeler, aka the Poo-bah
Courtesy of Curb Records

Rosie Carter (June's daughter).
Don't ever lose that smile, Rosie.

Rosie.

Friends

Dad and Billy Graham.

Me and Kris Kristofferson and the back of Waylon Jennings's head. This was at a "fifties-style" party that Waylon and his wife Jessi threw for Dad.

Larry Gatlin and me, Dallas Airport, 1982.

Dad and Waylon. My other Dad.

Dad and Bob Dylan, 1993.

I sang on the road for two years with Peggy Lynn (Loretta's daughter), Kathy Twitty (Conway's daughter), and Georgette Jones (George Jones and Tammy Wynette's daughter). We were called the Next Generation. It was a great concept, but we simply were not able to work together in harmony. I remain very close friends with Peggy Lynn today and speak to her often. It was a great experience and I had a lot of fun the two years the group was together.

Dad and George Jones. This is a classic!

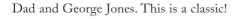

Peggy Lynn with our good friend Keith Watson. Keith was our sound technician and bodyguard on the road, and we've remained close friends.

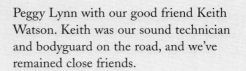

135

Open-Heart Surgery, 1989

December 19

Just six days until Christmas. It's 9:30 A.M. and my entire family is pacing Baptist Hospital while my father lies in the operating room undergoing a double bypass. We are all anxiously waiting for any news from the team of doctors responsible for Dad's life.

June is so tired, and everyone is relying on her to report any news of Dad's condition. She doesn't leave the hospital at all for the next eight days.

Finally, the doctors come in and tell us that everything went well and he's stable. We all thank God. You feel so helpless. All you can do is accept what the doctors tell you—no matter what it is. I want to be with him so bad, but so do my sisters and my brother. At this time June is the only one allowed in to see him.

I know in my heart that I am not prepared to accept any bad reports from the doctors. He must come through this with flying colors. I'll accept nothing else.

The thought of his life being taken away is beyond my comprehension. He will survive.

December 22

There are complications. He has pneumonia only three days after surgery. They put him back on the life support system and tell me I can see him for two minutes. Can I handle this? Rosanne and I ask to see him. I'm terrified. He's always been the indestructible man. I can't bear the idea of seeing him weak and helpless. I stand outside his room and compose myself to pull back the curtain. Rosanne has already gone in and June is comforting me and asking me not to cry. I do not. I pull back the curtains and see the machine is breathing for my father and he is not there. He is unaware. I can't look anymore. I step out. His hand is cold. I just want to go out. Please, God, don't let him die. Please, God, make him well again. Give him another chance.

December 22 (at night)

Waylon Jennings, Dad's best friend, has just had open-heart surgery the week before. His room is at the end of the hall from Dad's still "empty" room.

After I leave Dad's bedside, I have to breathe. I need to be alone for a minute. I can't stop crying. I've never seen Dad so lifeless. I'm sitting on the couch praying. I hear a dragging sound coming from down the hall. What is it? Whoever it is, they're moving very slow. I look up and there stands Waylon. His first time out of bed and he's pulling his IV stand behind him.

I say, "Waylon, what are you doing out of bed?"

He says, "I heard you crying."

I tell him to go back to bed, that I'll be all right, but he sits down beside me and puts his arm around me.

I'm still crying and he says, "Honey, your dad's going to be just fine. He's too mean to die."

We both laugh and for some reason, at that moment I know Dad will make it.

December 23

Sixth floor, Baptist Hospital. I'm sitting on a couch in the living room of the two-room suite that is to be my dad's room. As of today, he has yet to occupy this room. He is still on the fourth floor in the Intensive Care Unit recovering from open-heart surgery. This suite is waiting for him when he is well enough. In the meantime, it stays pretty full of family and friends, and people stopping by to visit and check on the latest condition of Dad.

Christmas Eve

The doctors come in and tell us that he is out of the woods. He will live. Thank you, God. Merry Christmas. The best gift ever.

Dad, you're going to live. Take good care of yourself.

Dad.

Tara, Rosanne, Kathy, and me: a winning combination.

Me, Dad, Tara, and the Cash family smile.

And the Winner Is . . .
Timex

A walk in the woods.

Dad is not a fancy man. He's most comfortable in his blue jeans and a cotton shirt, hanging out in his one-room cabin in the woods by his home. He's definitely happier drinking a big glass of buttermilk and eating corn bread than having a cup of tea served in expensive china.

His favorite store is K mart, not Bloomingdale's. He'd much rather be in his four-wheel drive than his Mercedes and he'd much rather be fishing than lunching at a country club.

He's much more concerned about how God sees him than about how others see him, and because of this, others look at him with great admiration.

I dropped in to see him one day. He'd just woken up from a nap and was about to get dressed. He said he couldn't find the watch he'd been wearing. He has a small safe in the office at his home and he was sitting on the floor in his pajamas taking all of his watches out of the safe. None of them would work, and every one of them was worth a few thousand dollars. We both just started laughing when he pulled out an old Timex and it was keeping perfect time.

Dad's Artwork

Skinny Mouse

Johnny Cash

More Photos from the Cash Family Album

All Grown Up

Dick and Mom on their twenty-fifth wedding anniversary.

My mom's brother, Ray Liberto, with his wife, Sammi. I am very close to them both and always have been, just as I am to my mom's sister, Sylvia, and her three daughters, Terri, Susan, and Jennifer.

John Carter.

Me and Dad swimming
at his house, 1992.

Rosanne and Rodney's wedding day. I've always loved this picture. L to R: Rosanne, Dad, Tara, me, and Kathy.

Jessica, 1995. My little beauty.

Me and Jerry Sharp.

Jessica at her high school graduation, June 1995.

Dustin (Kathy's son) at John Carter's wedding, June 1995.

Tara and Fred, shortly after their wedding.

Rosanne, Kathy, Mom, Tara, and me.

Me.

Kathy.

Jimmy Tittle (Kathy's husband, and my good friend).

Thomas (Kathy's son) with Chamisa, his new bride, 1996.

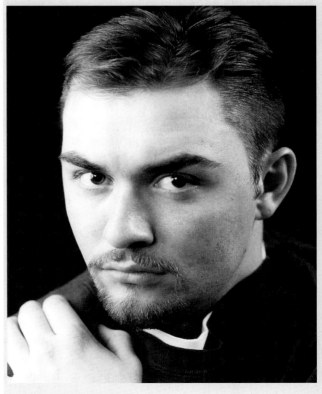

Thomas. He is a policeman today and we're all very proud of him.

Kacy (Kathy's daughter).

June, 1996.

Aran (Tara and Fred's son), the sweetest little boy in the world.

John Carter and
Mary's wedding
day, June 1995.

Hannah, Tara, and Jessica at Dad's house, 1994.

The Farm. This is Dad's favorite place in the world. It's the first place he goes when he gets home from a tour. It's about forty-five miles from his house in Hendersonville, out in the country. He goes here to find solitude, to write, or just to be alone with nature. He didn't even have a phone installed until 1988. Sometimes he'll call me from the Farm and ask me to drive down and cut his hair. We'll sit on the front porch while I cut his hair, then I'll get my metal detector out and we'll search for treasures.

Rosanne and John Leventhal on their wedding day, May 1995.

Rosanne and me, Memphis.

Me and Kathy.

Tara and Fred.

John Carter, me, Kathy, and Tara
at Dad's house, 1992.

Fred reading to Aran, who is holding his cat, Betty.

This is a photo of the House of Cash, Inc. It has been Dad and June's office, gift shop, and museum for more than twenty-seven years (since 1969). Dad closed the doors to the gift shop and museum on August 1, 1995. It was a very sad day for everyone involved, family and otherwise. Dad's reason was that he wanted to simplify his life and, as he put it, "travel a little less and spend more time with my grandchildren." He still conducts all his business from here, but it is no longer open to the public.

The Name "Cash"

RESEARCHED BY JOHNNY CASH

The name "Casche" originated in Scotland in the eleventh or twelfth century. The name apparently was taken by Ada, sister of King Malcolm the Fourth. King Malcolm and Ada lived in a castle on the Miglo River in County Fife, Scotland. When Ada left the castle to marry Casche, she was given the fertile lands east of the Miglo River. The lands along the river were later called Wester Cash, and those across the river, Easter Cash. When England conquered Scotland, the name was later changed and spelled Cash, as it sounded to the English, Casche being the original Gaelic spelling. The name means "the people who live in the king's house." Nothing remains of the castle of King Malcolm the Fourth. Some of the stones that were in the castle now make up the clock tower in the town of Strathmiglo. This town is just a few miles from Falkland Castle, which is a historic castle of the sixteenth and seventeenth centuries.

William Cash the First was a mariner who owned a ship called *The Good Intent,* and for many years until 1667, he plowed the seas back and forth from Edinburgh to the thirteen colonies, bringing Pilgrims to America. In 1667, he retired, bought a house and lot on Essex Street in Salem, Massachusetts, and settled down. He turned *The Good Intent* over to William Cash the Second, who continued the journeys across the Atlantic for many years. William Cash the Second settled in Westmoreland County, Virginia, in 1677. The Cash line moved from Westmoreland County to Stafford County and Amherst County, Virginia, during the 1700s. The direct line: John Cash, a Revolutionary War soldier, came to Georgia in 1802 from Bedford County, Virginia. Moses, son of John, lived in Elbert County, Georgia, and Reuben, born in 1814, came to Arkansas in an ox-drawn wagon in 1858. The Cash family lived in Cleveland County, Arkansas, until 1935, when Ray Cash moved to Dyess, Arkansas, before finally settling in Tennessee in 1969.

THE CASH FAMILY GENEALOGY

WILLIAM CASH

Immigrant ancestor born in Scotland in 1653. Wife Elizabeth. Settled in Westmoreland County, Virginia, 1677. Died 1708. St. Paul's Parish Book records Elizabeth's death on March 9, 1750, in Stafford County, Virginia, while apparently residing there with son Peter Cash. William Cash had eight children.

ROBERT HOWARD CASH

Son of William Cash, born in 1703. Married wife Ruth in 1724. Robert Howard Cash had eleven children.

STEPHEN CASH

Son of Robert Howard Cash, born in 1727. Wife Johanna. Died in June 1799, Amherst County, Virginia. Stephen Cash had eight children.

JOHN CASH

Son of Stephen Cash, born on April 5, 1757, Amherst County, Virginia. Married Lucy Campbell January 23, 1782. He was a Revolutionary War soldier. Came to Georgia in 1802 from Bedford County, Virginia. Died August 13, 1836, Henry County, Georgia. Lucy died January 23, 1848 in Pike County, Georgia. John Cash had seven children.

MOSES CASH

Son of John Cash, born in 1783 in Virginia. Married Nancy Hudson September 6, 1808. Married Nancy Craft Hunt July 6, 1824. Died July 6, 1845, Elbert County, Georgia. Moses Cash had twelve children.

REUBEN CASH

Son of Moses Cash, born in 1814, Elbert County, Georgia. Married Pheletis White Taylor February 11, 1836 in Elbert County. Moved to Arkansas in 1858 from Elbert County, in a wagon drawn by oxen. Died in Cleveland County, Arkansas. Buried in Cherry Cemetery on the Mt. Elba Road. Reuben Moses Cash had twelve children.

WILLIAM HENRY CASH

Son of Reuben Cash, born on July 27, 1852 in Elbert County, Georgia. Married Sarah Rebecca Overton October 1, 1874. She was born August 1, 1855, the daughter of John Henry Woodson and Susan W. Wharton Overton, and died June 16, 1916. William Henry Cash died December 3, 1912. Both were buried in the Overton–Cash Cemetery near the farm owned by J. H. W. Overton, below Toledo, Arkansas. William Henry Cash had twelve children.

RAY CASH

Son of William Henry Cash, born on May 13, 1897 in Rison, Arkansas. Married Carrie Rivers August 18, 1920 in Kingsland, Arkansas. She was born March 13, 1904 in Kingsland and died March 11, 1991. Ray Cash died December 23, 1985 and is buried at Woodlawn East, Hendersonville, Tennessee. Ray and Carrie Cash had seven children.

THE FAMILY OF RAY AND CARRIE RIVERS CASH

ROY CASH   (September 2, 1921–July 8, 1993)
     Married Claire Wandene Pickens (died August 23, 1985)
       i.   Roy Cash, Jr. (December 31, 1939)
       ii.   Jan Cash Bibb (January 20, 1942)
       iii.   Jackie Cash Murray (March 11, 1947)
       iv.   Gloria Jean Cash (December 17, 1948)
       v.   Larry Cash (January 23, 1944–May 1947)
       vi.   Darla Rae Cash Millichamp (June 3, 1964)

MARGARET LOUISE CASH
     Married Louis Fielder
       i.   Damon Earl Fielder (August 30, 1943)
     Married Jordan Garrett
       i.   Margaret Jo Garrett Klenk (December 30, 1946)
       ii.   Mike Scott Garrett (November 16, 1950)
       iii.   Paul Brent Garrett (August 24, 1962)

JACK DEMPSEY CASH   (November 1, 1929–May 20, 1944)

J. R. CASH, AKA JOHNNY CASH (February 26, 1932)
     Married Vivian Liberto
       i.   Rosanne Cash Leventhal (May 24, 1955)
       ii.   Kathleen Cash Tittle (April 16, 1956)
       iii.   Cindy Cash (July 29, 1958)
       iv.   Tara Joan Cash Schwoebel (August 24, 1961)
     Married June Carter
       i.   John Carter Cash (March 3, 1970)

REBA ANN CASH   (January 28, 1934)
     Married Donzil Burlison
       i.   Donny Wayne Burlison (November 19, 1950)
       ii.   Ricky Lynn Burlison (April 28, 1953–November 27, 1989)
     Married Donald Gene Hancock
       i.   Timothy Paul Hancock (September 11, 1962)
       ii.   Kelly Leigh Hancock (June 17, 1964)

JOANNE CASH   (March 9, 1938)
     Married Billy Ingle
       i.   Charlotte Ingle (July 7, 1957)
       ii.   Jeff Ingle (December 11, 1961)
       iii.   Rhonda Ingle Ponessa (September 15, 1963)
     Married Harry Yates

TOMMY CASH   (April 5, 1940)
     Married Barbara Wisenbaker
       i.   Mark Cash (May 18, 1962)
       ii.   Paula Cash Prutchnicki (October 2, 1963)
     Married Pamela Yvonne Dyer

$\mathcal{T}$oday

$\mathcal{T}$oday Dad is still as busy as ever. He does about two hundred show dates a year, along with TV specials, commercials, and guest shots; his most recent appearances were on Lorenzo Lamas's weekly show "Renegade" and "Dr. Quinn, Medicine Woman." He's currently recording an album, which will be released by the time this book is out. I believe that Dad will stay just as busy as he always has as long as he is able to.

My mother does not work a regular job but is as active as anyone I know. She's always been involved with many church activities and is still as involved as ever. She's the president of the San Buenaventura Garden Club, and Dick and she host the line dancing group at their church weekly and thoroughly enjoy it. She adores gardening and truly has a green thumb. She also loves to do interior decorating, crafting, and crocheting and is involved with many charitable organizations.

Her priority is her children and grandchildren. She still sends my sisters and me "care packages" every week and every holiday. Easter, Christmas, and even Valentine's Day, she sends us homemade chocolate in different shapes (hearts on Valentine's Day, bunnies on Easter, and so on).

I don't know where she finds the time, but she does. All the grandchildren and children also receive cards and gifts every holiday and birthday. She's an incredible lady and I'm very grateful for her.

My brothers-in-law stay busy as well. John, Rosanne's husband, produces albums, including those of many well-known rock performers such as Shawn Colvin, Marc Cohn, and Patty Larkin, along with some of Rosanne's recent work.

Jimmy, Kathy's husband, is an extremely fine singer and songwriter. He is currently under contract to Dixie Frog Records and his albums are being released in Europe. Several of his songs have appeared on other artists' albums, including a number he cowrote with Rosanne titled "On the Surface," which is on her album "Interiors." He also produces other new and up-and-coming artists. If I ever do another album, I would definitely ask Jimmy to produce it.

Fred, Tara's husband, has been an art director in the film industry for fifteen years. He also loves renovating older houses for resale and is into outdoor activities like backpacking, cross-country skiing, and gardening.

Tara is living in Oregon with Fred and their son, Aran. She stays very busy with her son, who is two years old now and discovering everything. She also works when she can as a wardrobe stylist in the film industry.

Kathy stays very busy with her two children, Dustin and Kacy. She is also an avid collector of celebrity memorabilia and makes a business out of reselling things she collects. Every week she donates her time to teach children and adults to read. She has done much research on literacy for this purpose.

Rosanne is still writing books and songs and recording albums and being Mom to her three daughters. She now lives in New York City.

John Carter has a talent for songwriting unlike anyone I've ever known. He is very much into writing new songs daily, which he performs locally and abroad. He is also busy, along with his wife, Mary, being a proud new parent since the birth of his son, Joseph, born February 25, 1996, one day before our dad's sixty-fourth birthday.

June still travels with Dad. She never misses a show and is still as funny and entertaining as ever. She is currently working on a book of fiction titled *Valerie Victoria*. I have read parts of it and believe it will be thoroughly enjoyed by anyone who reads it.

My stepfather, Dick, is a full-time travel agent. He takes good care of my mother, for which I am very grateful.

As for me, outside of working on this book off and on for many years, I have traveled on the road with Dad; I have recorded one album, independently, which I sell on the road; I worked at Dad's office for two years as mail-order manager and also organized and answered Dad's fan mail, which, by the way, pours in daily and kept me very busy. Dad always wanted every letter read and responded to. He would personally answer many letters.

I have been a professional makeup artist and hairstylist since 1982. I do makeup for TV commercials, album covers, and videos and I always do Dad's makeup when he is filming something locally. I also work full-time, unless I am called to do makeup, at a full-service salon, where I am a master barber. As you can see, I have a full life. Even so, every now and then I still get the urge to hit the road, and when I do, I jump on the bus with Dad and go. With my daughter, Jessica, having started college in September 1995, I may begin to go on the road more frequently.

I've worked on this book for so long, and have attempted in it to answer a lot of the questions I've been asked all my life. It has been a real pleasure and a great source of pride to put the book together; I hope you have enjoyed it and that it has given you some insight into my family and my dad.

At times, I feel my heart could nearly explode from the wonder of it all.

You look great, Dad.

*M*y Dad Today

To Cindy
With all my love
Dad

June took this recent photo of Dad. She gave it to me for Christmas in 1995.

The End

Alone now in silence

I know the time has come

To explore the things I feel

knowing all's been said and done

I'm immersed in what I feel

To live amongst it all

My guardian angel's at my side

Now I simply heed the call

There's a calm and quiet peace

In my body, mind, and soul

For myself, and all I love

I feel comfort, I am whole

CINDY CASH—JULY 31, 1996

Photograph Credits

Grateful acknowledgment is made to the following for permission to reprint photographs contained in *The Cash Family Scrapbook*: Karen Adams, Scott Brian Bonner, Jessica Brock, Kelly Mitchell Brown, John Carter Cash, June Carter Cash, Tara Cash-Schwoebel, Kathy Cash-Tittle, Hannah Crowell, Rodney Crowell, Dick Distin, Vivian Distin, Ron Keith, Winifred Kelley, Vicki Langdon, John Leventhal, Rosanne Cash Leventhal, James McGuire, Melody McKinley, Alan Messer, Gary Moor, Fred Schwoebel, Jerry Sharp, Marty Stuart, Bill Thorup, Dustin Tittle, and Jimmy Tittle.

The following photos—pages 75, Me and Carl Perkins; 97, Me and Rosanne in Jamaica; 133, Larry Gatlin and me; 150, Rosanne and me, Memphis—© Marty Stuart Collection.